Praise for Meg Losey

"As the frequency of life increases, we are seeing through the surface of an outworn reality into secrets and treasures of the past that have long been buried in the collective unconscious. Reintegrating this esoteric knowledge in light of the rapid transformation happening today is key. In *The Secret History of Consciousness*, Meg Blackburn Losey takes us on a fascinating tour of our forgotten wisdom, jumpstarting our memory as she goes. Then she helps us apply it to the shift of awareness that is fast occurring inside each one of us, to make change easier. A fascinating read full of riveting information!"

—Penney Peirce, expert intuitive and author of
Frequency: The Power of Personal Vibration and
The Intuitive Way: The Definitive Guide to Increasing Your Awareness

"Dr. Meg Blackburn Losey shows us how we can step out of the illusion of separation and into the greater truth of our multi-dimensional existence and our intimate connection to all life everywhere. This book is a very timely and significant contribution in these accelerated times as we race towards 2012 and beyond. The veils are lifting, and as we take back our creative powers we have an opportunity to completely redefine what it means to be human! This book speaks to that possibility."

—Bob Frissell, Flower of Life facilitator and author of
Nothing In This Book Is True, But It's Exactly How Things Are

The Secret History of Consciousness

The
Secret History
of Consciousness

Ancient Keys to Our Future Survival

MEG BLACKBURN LOSEY, PH.D.

WEISERBOOKS
San Francisco, CA / Newburyport, MA

First published in 2010 by
Red Wheel/Weiser, LLC
with offices at:
500 Third Street, Suite 230
San Francisco, CA 94107
www.redwheelweiser.com

Library of Congress Cataloging-in-Publication Data

Losey, Meg Blackburn.
The secret history of consciousness : ancient keys to our future survival
/ Meg Blackburn Losey.
p. cm.
Includes bibliographical references (p).
ISBN 978-1-57863-461-3 (alk. paper)
1. Consciousness–Miscellanea. 2. Cosmology–Miscellanea. I. Title.
BF1999.L635 2010
130–dc22   2010017531

Cover and text design by Kathryn Sky-Peck
Cover montage uses photography from Getty Images
Typeset in Goudy Old Style

Printed in the United States of America
TS
10 9 8 7 6 5 4 3 2 1
Text paper contains a minimum of
30% post-consumer-waste material.

Dedication

To Travis, Haley, Josh, and Devyn, my heart.

And to the Ancients who walked this earth long before us,
who left us everything we need to discover our true nature of being.

Acknowledgments

In researching this book I came to realize more and more that our predecessors gave us far more than we ever realized. In each sacred site there are similar clues that lead us to our very origin. To all of them, my eternal gratitude. Our paths to discovery would have been much longer without them.

To my readers, without you I would have very little to do. From my heart, thank you for all of the years of your dedicated feedback, emails, letters, and especially for all of the great hugs we share upon meeting.

To everyone at Red Wheel/Weiser, particularly to Jan for believing in me time after time, and to Bonni, Rachel, Donna, Susie, and all of the amazing staff there. Thank you.

To my agent and friend, Devra Ann Jacobs. There isn't anything we can't talk about. Thank you for believing in me all of these years.

And to David. You know already.

Contents

Introduction

The human experience appears to be a complex enigma, subject to everyday influences that contribute to what we do, feel, know, think we know, and believe, as well as how we actually live our lives. We use everything and everyone around us as reflections of ourselves to tell us if we are succeeding, if we fit in, if we have done a good job, and even to measure our happiness.

As we use external measures to mirror our experiences, we also become stagnant, stuck in our everyday lives, with only imaginings toward greater experiences to keep our hopes up that *someday* things will change.

We tend to believe only in what we can experience with our five senses—what we can see, hear, taste, feel, and smell. We have a hard time wrapping our minds around the possibility that there is more to our reality than what our five senses can measure. It is this limited perspective that keeps us mired in our illusions. It is our illusions of everyday life that are the real insanity as we dream our way through it all, judging, comparing, imagining our reality and then shaping our very being to fit what we decide is real. That is our mind talking. It has to understand. But we don't have to understand anything. We are unlimited in scope and possibilities.

Some of us have a sixth sense that we use to intuit the past, the future, and even things that are happening in the now. Those intuitions generally come as flashes of insight that intrude on our thoughts of the moment, startling us into a possibility that we hadn't considered. Where do those flashes come from? Can they be controlled or brought on intentionally?

Like the ebb and flow of the tides, periods of mass expanded consciousness appear to escalate and wane over time. Even through periods of lesser consciousness, some individuals manage to maintain or find their ways into these states of being. These individuals are either considered to be spiritual masters in their own rights, or people fear them, not understanding that the only difference between themselves and these conscious individuals is how much they are aware of realities beyond the obvious.

For instance, during the Inquisition, a very dark period in consciousness and history, people were massacred for not only their beliefs, but also their demonstrations of expanded consciousness. Joan of Arc is one of the best-known examples. In the early 15th century, she had visions and heard voices from other realms, which directed her toward a cause and gave her knowledge and clarity to the point that she actually led the king of France's army. Later, because Joan could not prove the source of her abilities, she was burned at the stake in 1431. Others have talked to God and seen angels and other entities that instructed them in the most holy aspects of being. Many of these people have been canonized as saints or revered across time as being wise ones, sages who hold the mysteries of the universe within them.

The Salem witch trials are another perfect example of a period of darkness of consciousness. In 1692, Puritan religious factions in early Salem, Massachusetts, hunted down people (mostly women) whom they believed to be witches doing the devil's work and burned them at the stake. Any excuse could be used to accuse someone of witchcraft, and there really wasn't any defense against the accusers. Mass hysteria created by Puritan values and fear of the devil led to one false accusation of witchcraft after another. Any denial by the accused was considered to be devil speak, and the accused was quickly brought to imagined justice by being burned at the stake. Either someone was a witch or they weren't. There was no middle ground or leeway for unfair accusations. One by one, and sometimes more than one at a time, innocent victims were burned alive under the fearful belief that they were a danger to society. Often, those who were accused and eliminated exhibited nothing more than a consciousness higher than that of their accusers.

Fear is generally the reason those with access to higher conscious awareness are persecuted. For example, Jesus of Nazareth was crucified because those in power believed that in some way he was a threat to the kingdom and, therefore, to those in political dominance and control at the time. He spoke of esoteric subjects using language and parables that fit the culture of the time. People followed him because they had an internal recognition of the truth in his words. They witnessed the miracles he performed and knew him to be truth, and yet others were threatened by him.

These examples and more are glimmers of evidence from throughout ancient history and even before, telling us that consciousness and intelligence are separate entities. Further, there is evidence that consciousness travels outside of the body, traversing the barriers between life and death; between dark and light; between the past, present, and future; and even between other-dimensional realities.

What did the ancients know that we do not? Why are we not always at the height of our awareness? Why at times throughout human existence did some civilizations seem to have great technologies and an inside track on infinite being? How did they know, for instance, how to create technologies for the distribution of power, for atomic processes, for utilizing harmonics to change the fabric of creation? How did the ancients know about alchemy, such as the manufacturing of monatomic gold in the form of white powder that could be ingested, thereby introducing a conductive material into the physical body that would heighten conscious awareness? Why was knowledge of this rite and other secrets limited to pharaohs, priests, kings, and wise men? What was hidden from the people at large? Exactly the same information that was taught to select apprentices at the mystery schools: access to higher consciousness led to altered and infinite reality.

In the first part of this book, we will explore evidence of ancient times and people. What the ancients left behind was every key that we need to know about who we are and what we are capable of. Once we have a grasp of the concepts the ancients left for us, we can learn how to apply them to this now.

For instance, when do people begin to realize that the possibilities of life are much greater than they had previously imagined? Is there an impetus, a moment in time, or some vast or tiny change inside of them that flips switches of awareness? Is this an individual happening, or does it occur across the populous of the planet? Does consciousness actually expand, or do we just reconnect with it?

Does our consciousness have anything to do with our creative processes? Do we create our own realities, or do we just live in the realities that we find ourselves in? Do we have the power to change our realities as individuals or as groups?

Is there a time when consciousness evolves and awareness becomes keener? If so, are we affected physically? Do our brains change in response? Does our DNA have some special coding or instruction contained within it that instigates or responds to higher awareness under certain circumstances? Does intelligence make us more consciously aware? Does conscious awareness make us more intelligent? Are there signs of impending awareness expansion, and if so, how can we recognize them?

Inherently, we are created to seek our source, to reconnect with our divinity, and yet in the current world condition, many of us feel empty, unfulfilled, even lost. We aren't even sure of what we believe because there is so much information available to us. We grasp at the tried and true, or we become immersed in religion, hoping that it will fulfill us, or we try every esoteric practice that comes along.

Inside, we feel a need to return home, but we can't seem to remember where home is. We want to feel emotional expansion to the depths of our being, but we have covered our emotions for so long that we aren't even sure how emotions *do* feel. We confuse our emotions with our mental perceptions and make our way rationally through our limiting thoughts. We seem to forget that we are capable of great depths of emotional experience. We become unhappy, dissatisfied, and bored, succumbing to the idea that this must be all there is. How sad is that?

What if we realized that it is all simple? We can. We can find that we are everything that we seek and that everything we seek also seeks us. What if we realized that we are capable of creating whatever reality we want, anytime, anywhere? What if we didn't just know we *could*? What if we *did*? In my experiences, I have found that it is all simple and that all chaos is nothing more than a series of simplicities that have become entangled.

The ancients knew these secrets, and now you will too. The consciousness of change is a very real state of being. It is not a gimmick. We don't have to buy anything. We already *are* the change!

The consciousness of change is our sense beyond our five physical senses, and it is even greater than our intermittent sixth sense. The consciousness of change leaps into the universal construct as our seventh sense. Our seventh sense is infinitely aware, even though we may not be conscious of that awareness. But what if we were? What are we missing? How can we open the door to our seventh sense, so that we can take advantage of all that creation has to offer us?

This book will teach you how the past, present, and future are intricately linked together and how pure consciousness has everything to do with change and creating reality. From there, it will explain just how powerful we are in our contributions to both ourselves and a much greater whole.

As the year 2012 approaches, there are a number of reasons that we are reawakening to the infinite possibilities available to us. Are planetary influences, subtle energies, the photon belt, and even interdimensional happenings contributing toward a great shift or change? What does a date in the future have to do with what we are experiencing now? Anything at all? Oh, yes. More than we realize.

Are the mysteries of consciousness unavailable, even forbidden, to us as mere mortals? Not at all. We simply have to remember what we already know: that we are the consciousness within the living One. We are actually running this show—all of us.

It is all simple, and together, we can explore how it works. It is my desire that the information, the tools, in this book will assist you by not only giving you new information, but experientially as well. I want you to know that you don't have to be a victim of life, that you are the god you seek. Yes, you are that powerful. The first step is awareness, and that is where this book comes in.

This isn't about magic or scary secret practices. It is a book of answers and possibilities. The secret is that there are no secrets, only infinite possibilities toward immeasurable outcomes. This is a book about the mysteries of consciousness, the blending of our humanity with our divinity, on purpose and on earth. As you, the reader, experience this book, open yourself to the possibility that maybe, just maybe, you aren't who you think you are. Maybe, just maybe, you are far greater than you could have imagined. Maybe, just maybe, what you believe isn't real. What you *know* is. Who you *are* is.

What you know sometimes takes a little remembering. These pages will remind you.

Included within this work are many graphics with symbols. These are some of the same symbols that my guides used to teach me and to adjust my energy field so that I could keep up with their teachings. Created of the original language, the language of light, these symbols are powerful initiations to information that is stored in our bodies as pure consciousness. They are keys to unlocking your infinite self. They are for your experience, to open within you possibilities that you may not have yet considered. Each one of the symbols is paired with a meditation to help you open your awareness of reality beyond the everyday illusion and into the infinite. As you access your inner awareness with the symbols, they will communicate with you energetically, consciously, and not at all mentally. Let yourself absorb the possibilities that are contained within each symbol. What comes of this experience will unfold within you over time and easily, if you let it.

From this moment forward, open your heart. Open your mind. Let go of everything that you believe and consider the possibilities of an even greater reality. You won't be disappointed!

I am grateful once again to bring you, the reader, new and exciting possibilities that can change old paradigms and beliefs into new experiences of fullness and greatness of living. Encountering this information is like taking a rocket ride with no seatbelts or shoulder straps. Go with the flow and never look back, for we are in an infinitely changing reality. And all of it is our creation!

The Secret History of Consciousness

Chapter One

Coming Out of the (Spiritual) Closet

The legends of King Arthur refer to a wonderful, whimsical, yet powerful wizard named Merlin, who "lived backwards." Most people would take that to mean that Merlin began as a very old man who became younger every year. But that wasn't it at all. Merlin found the doors to the infinite consciousness and then learned how to apply that vast knowledge to the comparatively narrow world of human comprehension and existence. What seemed to be feats of magic were nothing more than Merlin accessing realities beyond our familiar world.

I know, because I found those doors myself.

What I am about to tell you may sound very strange, but this story is quite real and the experiences are phenomenal. Moreover, every day, science is proving the resulting knowledge to be true, and that knowledge has had resounding effect across the planet and beyond.

Over the years, hundreds, if not thousands, of people have asked me to tell my story, and in most cases I have resisted, not wanting to seem like another "woo-woo" person with a great imagination. But during these years, the world has grown up, and I guess I have too. So here it goes.

Being intuitive has been natural for me my entire life. As a child in Catholic school, I really understood the meaning of *holy* and the inner place from which the saints' devotion came—that place in our heart of hearts where we can go to become unified with all things, that place inside of us that is our source connection, our link to the memories of all times and infinite possibilities from which we can create anything that we desire. That place that many people call the God within us. It can be an overwhelming place.

I remember one day as a child, when I was in my friend's playhouse, the air all of a sudden sort of snapped, crackled, and turned blue. I heard a rustle and saw a light that sprouted wings, unfolding as a dove that flew toward me and over my head as I ducked. "Hey!" I yelled at my friend, "Did you see the Holy Spirit just now?" (I mean, really, what else would you call it?) My friend just kind of shrugged and blew me off. She hadn't seen or heard a thing.

That experience was the beginning of many that no one else believed. Strange was normal for me. I knew things. From a very deep heart place, I understood what people felt, what they really meant when they said things, how much pain humanity carried. I seemed to be empathic to the emotional injuries of others and to have compassion for the pain that I saw and felt.

It became hard for me to tell the difference between their emotions and mine, so I shut off my intuitive understanding as best as I could. Deep down the awareness simmered, but I found a way to cover it up. When I was a teenager, alcohol and drugs provided a blissful escape, but ultimately I felt worse, as their effects lingered in my sensitive system. Later, I developed defensive behaviors and built walls a mile thick around my emotions. Yet all the while I still felt *everything*.

Because no one else seemed to have an awareness like mine, I hid my experiences, keeping them to myself. I tried really hard to be like everyone else, but I always had the feeling that I didn't fit in anywhere. For a couple of decades, I lived a cardboard life. I lived and loved from the perspective of those around me—my friends, my family, everyone. For example, when I asked my dad what it would take for him to be proud of me, for me to be a success, he said, "Do well in business." So I set out to prove to dad that I was made of that stuff, that I had the grit and determination of a successful business person.

There came a day in 1998 when my cardboard world—everything that I knew to be my life, the foundation of my reality—began to crumble. I found myself alone on my friend's sofa because I had nowhere else that felt safe. One morning, I woke up and was sobbing. At that moment, there wasn't a thought in my head, but I was enshrouded in pain. My heart was broken. Nothing made sense. The grief was alive and consuming me.

It was time to regroup. "Okay, self," I said, "We are not getting up off of this couch until we figure out what is going on here."

I began to look at my life with a fresh set of eyes. I looked at my role in every situation. What I saw was a rude awakening. I had become dishonest and manipulative with myself, and I had a sense of false bravado that I was some great success. I realized that all I was doing was blaming everyone else for my problems. It was time take responsibility for my own actions and perceptions.

As I looked in my own inner mirror, I also realized that I was in no way authentic. I had learned to cover up every deep feeling, every perception, and every little tiny bit of me there was. I had to get real. So I reached into my heart of hearts and said aloud to the otherwise empty room, "Whoever I am, whatever I am, I *accept*."

I can't emphasize enough the humility that went with that statement, what it meant to truly let go. The words rolled through my body like a tidal wave. I felt much lighter than I had only a moment before. From that moment forward I decided to live authentically, no matter what, to maintain the humility that brought me to getting real.

The first thing I learned was that I didn't know how to tell the truth. I don't mean I lied to everyone all of the time. I didn't know how to tell *myself* the truth, and because of that, I had become a pretty good B.S. artist with everyone else. But after that moment of humble acceptance, I began to practice truth. I caught myself when I was covering up what I really felt, and I began to learn how to feel safe revealing my more inner thoughts and feelings. Soon that spilled over into practicing on other people. I would swallow hard and speak the truth as I saw it. Funny thing was, as I did, people became more comfortable with me, and I with them. Simultaneously, the people in my life that really didn't fit, people with whom I'd had destructive relationships, started to just kind of fade into the sunset. But as each negative person fell away, others came into my life—others who were authentic and, even more exciting, open to the idea that what we see around us isn't the only reality there is in creation.

One day I ran into a tenant to whom I had leased a client's house in the middle of a gorgeous old farm. She invited me to come to her house for weekly group meetings she was having. She told me that the meetings were all about astrology, and that they did drumming and different things like that. The next week, I timidly wandered into the meeting. It was already in progress when I arrived. Everyone in the room was quiet except for a young woman in the back of the room. Her eyes were glazed, and her posture was kind of strange—stiff, like she wasn't comfortable in her body. My eyebrows must have gone up because someone seated near me whispered that the young woman was channeling. I had barely and only recently heard of channeling, and I wasn't even sure I believed in it. But I decided that if I were going to live authentically, I would stay out of judgment and give this experience a chance.

That experience was much more than chance. It was a door, and without realizing, I had walked right through it.

I continued going to the weekly meetings because the people who attended were wonderful, loving, and didn't seem to want anything from me. They honestly seemed to like me for me. It was a comfortable place— one where I had no ties, no strings, and I could learn to relate to people I didn't know from my new and authentic self. As I did, I started feeling energy in my hands; little squiggly spirals tickled the ends of my fingers. My palms were on fire. My intuition blew wide open. It was annoying at times because I would hear snips of people's thoughts, and I couldn't help it. I knew things—what would happen next, when it would happen, who would be there, everything.

I rediscovered that place inside of me that I knew so intimately as a child—that place I secretly called my holy place. When we did meditations at the meetings, I would automatically open my heart and move into that inner place I had found. I learned to stay in that place as long as I wanted. And as I accessed that place inside of me more and more, life began to get more and more comfortable—magical, in fact. I discovered that when I got out of my own way, life was really, really easy. Without realizing it, I was learning to live unconditionally.

Often, the young woman who had been channeling at the first meeting I'd attended would channel different entities, who gave very emotional messages to the group. During one such channeling, I was filled with so much energy that I felt as if I would explode. I could barely sit still. I was physically uncomfortable, and the intensity continued to grow. Worse, my throat felt strange. It felt full and as if it would speak of its own accord. I clamped my mouth shut so hard it hurt. I didn't want to blurt something out and embarrass myself and everyone else. I felt as if I was having a battle with an unseen force, and it was nearly winning. When the channeler had finished, I could take it no longer. After a barely respectable moment, I jumped out of my chair and started pacing back and forth in the small room. I told the channeler I didn't know what was happening, and I described the feeling I was having inside.

She very kindly said, "That's just how I felt when I first began to channel."

Uh oh, I thought. This was *not* where I'd thought I was headed. Could I really channel? Me?

The mother and daughter who hosted the weekly meetings offered to work with me to see what would happen. I was given great instructions about how to keep myself safe, how to let only those entities who were "of the light" enter my body.

When I first began stepping aside so that an entity could speak through me, I would hover next to myself, just outside of my body, watching, listening. Since I had become all about authenticity, I became really annoyed at myself for doing this. After all, something might be said through my body, with my face, that someone would take home and use. That message might change their life, and it would be my fault. However, when I voiced that concern out loud, I realized I was calling in the wisdom of God and then questioning his word. Who was I to doubt? From that moment forward, once I was comfortable with the incoming energies, I leaped right out of my body. I became a deep-trance channel to the point where people used to identify my channeling with the work of Edgar Cayce, the sleeping prophet.

One night at group, after I was finished channeling and returned to my chair, I looked over at the young man who was sitting across from me. His kidneys were failing, and the dialysis treatment he was having wasn't working. He was on a transplant list. As I looked at him, my vision switched to his insides—not just to his internal organs, but also to the tiniest inner workings of his physical being. It was beautiful and fascinating.

Spontaneously, I began to read his body to him, somehow explaining that the sodium content and some other things having to do with his dialysis weren't in the right balance for him. I saw it all, and told him everything. Around the room, everyone stopped in their tracks.

The information turned out to be right on. When the young man's dialysis was adjusted to the new protocol, he felt much better.

This new ability was exciting to me. As time went on, I found that the reads would happen spontaneously if someone asked a health question. This gift seems to be a natural ability, and since my first experience, it has expanded. Many medical doctors have taken my classes on interdimensional healing. One of them actually stood up in front of a class of about thirty people and told them I was better than an MRI. I had worked with his sister who had metastatic breast cancer, and I had read tiny lesions in her brain, exactly where they were later found.

In conjunction to the new sight I had gained, the intense energy in my body was relentless. I couldn't seem to find a trigger switch to let the energy out of me. I was losing weight and couldn't sleep. It was as if I were plugged into an invisible force that never stopped. In an effort to get more comfortable, I began to play with the energy. I'd put on music that had no real melody, and I'd begin to move, allowing the energy to flow through me, out of my hands, around me, inside of me. One day, as I spread my hands, my sight opened again, and I saw a rainbow-colored arc flowing from my right hand over my head to my left hand. I was in awe.

And then I got aggravated. I started talking out loud. "Okay, this is beautiful, but I have no idea what to do with it. So *now what?*" I had no clue, so I kept moving and kept working with the energy.

Every morning, I did the same thing, and out of desperation, I would say aloud to no one I could see, "Someone *show me* what to do!"

One morning someone showed up. An absolutely magnificent holographic being stood right there in front of me, in the middle of my living room. I was so startled I jumped straight up and straight back.

He disappeared.

Quickly, I centered myself and found the sacred place within me. I opened my eyes, and there he stood again, patiently waiting for me. He was grandly and extraordinarily tall, with very defined features. His hair was nearly black, and it flowed over his shoulders. He literally glowed in his crimson robes. In fact, he glowed seemingly from the inside out. He was almost transparent, but he felt huge and solid. Dear God, what was happening? I didn't know for sure, but I did know that all of those times I had begged for clarity, for help, for understanding, really had been heard.

The being started to move like I had been doing, but with some very subtle changes. As I watched him, the energy he manipulated changed color and shape. In my body, I could feel what was happening in his hands. I started to move too, mimicking him. As I did, the energy within my hands began to change shape and change color.

Every morning, as if by cosmic appointment, I met with this being, whom I had lovingly begun to refer to as "Master," because his presence felt like an expanded part of that holy place inside of me. His presence to me felt like sacredness embodied and oh, how humble I felt! Calling him Master seemed insufficient, almost trite, but yet there were no other words to describe him. Being with this Master reminded me of what it must be like to be in the presence of enlightened beings such as the group of Ascended Masters that included Jesus, Metatron, Enoch, and others. I grew to love these moments, when he and I would move together. Instead of feeling insane, I felt calmer and more centered than I ever had in my life. My inner vision had changed again and again, growing in scope and abilities. And all I kept saying was, "Show me." Never why, what, or who—just "Show me."

One day, as we were moving together, my entire sense of reality changed. It was as if I had leaped into another dimension or into someone else's dream. I found myself walking down a path, away from my cosmic teacher. As I walked down the path, a young boy came to me and said I had to go with him.

"No!" I firmly told him. I had to keep practicing.

The kid wouldn't take no for an answer. He looked like a peasant from 19th-century Europe. His blond hair was tousled, and his pants torn at the knees. His white shirt was at least two sizes too big and well worn, like a hand-me-down. Yet he spoke with such a confidence and authority that I couldn't ignore him. So I followed. Up the narrow path we climbed until we came to a large opening in the native rock. It was the entrance to a grotto, a shallow cave. In it were twenty or so men, all in white. They were silent, as if keeping vigil for something. Another man there held a sword, tip down, in the position of peace. He silently beckoned me with his liquid brown eyes.

"Listen," I said, "I have work to do, and I don't have time for distractions." He remained silent, yet I heard in my body that I was supposed to go to him. I did. There was a ceremony, and he gave me a gift, although I didn't understand it at the time.

At the moment the ceremony culminated, my sense of reality shifted again, and I was at the entrance to a courtyard. There was a gate in the arched entrance, but I couldn't go through it. My feet felt glued to the floor. I could see people in the courtyard beyond, milling about. I wondered what this place was. It felt like a university of some kind, but I wasn't sure.

A wizened old man sat at a table to my left, seeming to ignore me. His gray hair straggled limply down the sides of his head, and his thin beard lay folded atop his huge belly. His eyebrows were so bushy I could barely see his narrow brown eyes. The table was inlaid with azurite, malachite, lapis lazuli, tiger's eye, moonstone, and other semiprecious stones. I heard a voice inside of me say to look up. The energy had begun to well up in me, so with my eyes, I raised my hands, hoping to release the intensity. Instead, light came out of my hands to meet the bright light that had opened above me. As I began to move, the light took on shape and density. It became a carved object, and that object felt as real as cold carved stone. I explored the object and then, somehow knowing what to do, set it on the old man's table.

Each day I worked with this new Master, changing energy into geometric shapes, then forms, and soon the objects seemed to solidify in my hands. As they did, I would reach over and set them on the Master's table. He would never acknowledge me. It was maddening to me that he never spoke about what was happening. I wanted him to tell me I was doing a good job. I wanted him to tell me *anything*. Finally, I realized there was no need for his approval. I was simply learning. I didn't know what I was learning, but I knew something big was going on, and I was right in the midst of it.

Then, one day, as I reached my hands and my eyes up into the light, I saw the same dove I had seen as a child, hovering above me. I reached far into its light and felt something warm in my hand. As I brought my hand out of the light, I found myself holding a white dove. The light had solidified into this magnificent creature. Its breast was against the center of my palm. I could feel its heartbeat, smell its dander. Its warm breath tickled my thumb.

And I cried.

I was so overcome with emotion that I fell to my knees.

I held this little bird to my heart, and as I did the love within me grew to an indescribable volume. After being with this little miracle for a time, I lifted my hands back into the light and set him free. As he flew upward, he changed back into light.

I cried some more. It was so real. It had to be real. Would anyone else have seen it had they been there? What did it matter? I had found the doorway to the heavens, and my heart and soul had already leaped through it.

Not long after my second encounter with the dove, I found myself standing alone in a place that had no detail. There were no walls, no specific sources of light, just me. But as I looked around, I realized that my original Master was there. He reached out and covered me with a white cloak. I had no idea what that meant, except that things were about to change again.

Many days later, I decided to see what the white robe was about. Sitting in my favorite chair, I went into my now-familiar etheric, other-dimensional space and donned the robe. Immediately, I was in another reality—a terribly primitive one. Nearly naked men clamored toward an animal they had just brutally killed. The scent of fresh blood was overwhelming, and the men smelled so rank I could barely breathe. I started to move closer to see what was happening, what the men were doing, and all of a sudden, reality shifted again.

I was in another time, another place, *inside of a huge tree*. There, three old crones, all in rough, gray and brown pinafores that reminded me of flour sacks, sat at a table. They were giggling as they watched a curved wooden fish rock back and forth in front of them.

Then *whoosh!* Again reality shifted, and I was somewhere else, then somewhere else. I was jumping time and space! I was literally visiting other times and places. And the people in each new setting *could see me!*

The morning after that initial dizzying series of trips, I sat down in my favorite chair again. As I entered into the unlimited realms of consciousness, I found myself in a room that seemed to have no walls. I felt as if I was somewhere before time as we know it. No matter how far I reached with my awareness, I could identify no boundaries. A holographic pyramid hovered all around me, and I saw myself inside of it. At the same time, I saw myself about twenty feet away, watching myself. And all that time, I was aware of myself standing in my living room. There were three of me and I realized that I had gone multidimensional.

Inside the pyramid chamber, a new Master came. His robes were violet, he felt older than time, and as he moved, the light he emitted trailed behind him. He told me he was from the before times—the times before the earth was formed and before the people who came before us inhabited the earth. He showed me a time and place so far back I had no point of reference for it.

We stood within the light of the pyramid that surrounded us. Before us was a table with someone on it, but I couldn't seen enough detail to know who it was. Together the new Master and I began to work with energy in an entirely new and different way. He stepped inside of my body. As I looked down at my arms, they were no longer mine—they were the Master's. As we worked in unison, my mentor had me feel the energy of he and I combined as well as the energy inside of the person on the table. My new Master showed me, in geometric patterns, how the energy was transmuting into a completely changed form. We were literally changing the energy field of the person on the table, harmonizing it, altering the frequencies of the energies, the shapes, and even the way the different energies related to each other.

At one point the Master stepped back and my attention was directed fully to the person on the table. I was startled to see that we had been working on yet another dimensional version of me! Then I stood behind myself watching myself working on myself. Needless to say, this was getting a bit confusing. Was I really all that? Was I none of it? I decided that the questions didn't matter; only what I saw and learned did.

This was true interdimensionality. I felt as if I had finally gone home.

Over many sessions together, this Master took me into many other chambers and taught me vastly about energy and healing. He took me to one chamber with a table that looked like a great alabaster slab. As I looked at the table, a body materialized above it. The body was transparent and began to rotate. I saw areas inside of the body that were dark, not light and airy like the rest of the body. The Master showed me how to command change in the body. Just as I had done with the previous Master in the courtyard, I reached into the light, and the energies changed form. I was learning about harmonic dysfunction in the human body.

The Master took me to another chamber that looked like it had pillars all around it and a depressed area in the floor at the center. Other Masters stood between the pillars. In my head I heard the words, "Holding the energy." Then I heard, "This is one of the healing chambers of what you call Atlantis."

From the floor all around the depression shot arcs of energy. Full-color spectrums of light arched from one side to the other across a body that laid in the depression in the floor. I immediately understood. The body was becoming retuned. The color spectrums were affecting the entire body, and the energy of the body was responding. Again I had the understanding that the body in the chamber was me and that in my experience I was absorbing libraries of healing and knowledge. Some part of me was beginning to understand what was going on with this entire set of experiences.

During subsequent visits, several more Masters came and went. It seemed that each of them brought me a new piece of the cosmic puzzle, an etheric education that defied all logic or cognizance. Once I had a great grasp of geometry and color and energy relations, they began to show me how all of those things were related to the creation of reality and matter. Later they showed me how, within the form of creation, consciousness travels and new realities are created. The lessons never ceased. I found myself knowing about sciences that I had never studied. I became more and more capable of reaching my consciousness out into the ether for virtually any kind of information, and even more astounding, I actually began to comprehend the meaning of the experiences. The pieces of the puzzle came together as a body of knowledge that was infinite and fully accessible.

One morning toward the end of the intense succession of Masters, I entered into interdimensional awareness and found myself standing at a water's edge, watching the most beautiful Master I had ever seen. He was in robes that overlapped in cobalt and sky blues. He shimmered, and he, even more than the other Masters, felt like that holy place inside of me that was so familiar. I knew he was the embodiment of love. He stood silently and waited for me to get his message. Instantly and without effort, I moved across the water to stand behind him. I reached around his waist, and I *stepped into him!*

I had graduated.

The Master then took me into a new chamber and handed me what looked like a golden chalice. On its stem were intricately carved symbols. I had never seen anything like them. As I looked at them, the symbols seemed to fill me with something beyond thought, beyond words. They were filling me with knowledge.

Taking the cup into my hand, I looked inside. It was filled with liquid light.

"Drink of this," the Master said.

I did.

A strange peace washed through me. I knew that whatever had just happened, life was never going to be the same again. After my graduation, on a daily basis, nearly everything that I thought became reality. I experienced a clarity about every aspect of creation, from the tiniest to the largest. My consciousness could reach into the ethers for any kind of information I desired, even on subjects I knew nothing about. *I had consciously and willingly entered into the infinite.*

As I worked with my new knowledge, the tools that I had been given, and the skills that I had been taught by the Masters, I seemed to move instantly through time and space. Consciously traveling through the cosmos, I saw planets born, stars explode, planets change their elliptical patterns. I gained understanding of black holes, parallel realities, and dimensions; I began to learn the shortcuts through time and space via wormholes and stargates, in form and function. As I travelled through the cosmos, I saw geometric shapes—cubes, rectangles, pyramids, and more. I got the feeling they were doorways. Once I walked through one of these holographic shapes and discovered it was a portal to knowledge. Through that portal, I learned about light and harmonics, color and frequencies, geometry and its relations to everything in creation. I learned that light has memory. Light actually never, ever forgets. And I learned why and how.

Outside of my training with the Masters, I was still participating in the metaphysical group that I had earlier so timidly joined. Months had gone by, the seasons had changed from the beginning of spring to fall and then winter. I had lost my concept of "earth time" as my travels in other realities had taught me that time truly doesn't exist except in our perceptions. At about this time, individual entities stopped coming through me when I channeled and a higher frequency group consciousness began to speak through me. It wasn't one being; it was a group of beings. They called themselves the A Lan Ta. They said that was the true name of Atlanteans. They were very powerful and serious. Listening to the tapes of the A Lan Ta is like listening to intergalactic lessons in consciousness. Over about eight weeks, the group of beings taught me about the structure of the pyramid, its meaning, the universal relationship between pyramids and all of creation, and about much more. When they were finished, they were gone.

The A Lan Ta were followed by an even more high-frequency group of beings. The new group had no name. They said that to define them with words is an untruth because they, like us, are infinite beings. This group remains with me even now. Shortly after the new group appeared, they began filling my head with many of the symbols that you will experience in this book. Often I would see the symbols rain down over me or over the person with whom I worked on the healing table. Each symbol is like a library unto itself. Each contains measureless amounts of messages that will fill you energetically with information more ancient than time. It is impossible to form a cognitive meaning for any of them. They are beyond words, and they are exquisite. They are, as I say, initiation and instruction by osmosis.

My "guys," as I call the group, are loving and hilarious, serious and the epitome of love. They are both male and female in their presence and have never had the experience of inhabiting a physical body—they are beings of light. They have remained with me for nearly ten years now, guiding me, teaching me, and often exasperating me as they interrupt me either in my thoughts or while I am teaching. They speak in my mind, appear once in a while to make a point, or take me to places in other realities. Sometimes they wake me up at night, standing near my bed and pushing at me with their energy fields. We have come to a balance with each other that allows me to have my much-needed human experiences while they guide and teach me about things beyond this world at the same time. The Masters who taught me in the beginning, and others who now come and go to speak both to me and through me, are all truth embodied. When I leave my body so that they can speak through me, I find myself among them, part of their collective consciousness. They have brought so much information to us over the past ten or so years that I can't possibly remember it all. Further, they are always right.

Over time, I've discovered that when I have learned new and amazing things that I don't really understand, someone—a human being who I don't know at all, but who is exactly the right person to share the information with—comes to me.

For example, just after the Masters gave me new and different information about genetics and the inner workings of DNA, a geneticist came to visit me. She was a beautiful soul. She came to my home, sat in a chair in my living room, and shook her head.

"I have no idea why I am here," she said.

"What do you do?" I asked.

"I am a geneticist," she replied.

I nearly jumped out of my chair. When I shared my visions with her (my terminology was not great, but my descriptions were good enough that she understood me completely), she asked me how I knew what I was telling her. Apparently, part of the information I gave her had been published in a genetics journal just that week. She was excited about the information and believed what I was telling her was real and true. So I told her about what was coming next in the field of genetics—about changes in our DNA strands, how the segments in the strands will begin to interrelate and many to date unused segments will begin waking up and becoming active. I also told her what I saw in our future, as the relationships within and across DNA strands will be changing as well as increasing in electromagnetic emissions from the strands themselves.

One week a man came to our group. He told me that he had heard about my experiences, and he wanted me to speak at the conference he was producing. I was at once excited and terrified, but in those moments, a speaker was born. The day of my talk, I was worried that when I began to tell my story, people would walk out on me. After all, the story I had to tell was beyond bizarre, even to me. Instead, as I talked, the audience was riveted. And when the hour was over, no one moved. They wanted more. I realized that people were hungry for the kind of information I had to share.

When people began to find out what I knew, what effects interdimensional healing could have—like heart valves spontaneously repairing themselves, tumors disappearing, lives changing dramatically and instantly—my life was no longer my own. People began to flock to me, wanting me to fix them. I tried and tried to help them understand that they could fix themselves, and still they came. Realizing the gifts that I had found in myself were not for me to hide, but for the world, I found it hard to say no. I eventually got hung up in that messianic place of thinking that my life was indelibly not mine any more. I remember thinking, "What about me?"

The thought made me very sick.

In 2003, I found a lump in my breast that turned out to be a huge mass of cancer—stage three and growing like a wild fire. The tumor was larger than my fist and had grown to within 2 millimeters of my chest wall. According to medical doctors, the prognosis was grim. But I knew I could fix it. I had all of the tools, right? But just in case, I called everyone that I knew who was adept at alternative healing, and the night before my surgery was scheduled, we all met in the ethers and worked together. The morning of my surgery, I awoke to find that the tumor was still there. I found that really hard to believe, but there it was, and there I was living a nightmare that was only beginning.

"I guess this is mine to experience," I remember thinking courageously. So I went through a devastating surgery that left me ravaged and what I considered to be permanently mutilated. But the doctors were amazed to see that instead of growing into my lymph glands or further out into the tissues of my chest, the tumor had encapsulated. It had been enclosed in a wall of tissue, and even though it was over 7 inches long and 5 inches wide, it had not spread anywhere else. "Well," I thought, "we *did* get it handled, didn't we?"

Despite successfully removing the entire tumor, my doctors still told me to expect the worst. They were certain that with a cancer as aggressive as mine had been, I didn't stand much chance of it not recurring. After they nearly killed me with the first few treatments of chemotherapy, I had had enough. I told them I would take care of any further cancer *my* way.

And I did. Now, many years later, I am alive and healthy, with no residual effects from the cancer and no reoccurrence. After the initial surgery and treatments, we moved to another state, and after several years of regular checkups, my new doctor was awed that the cancer hadn't returned. He actually confessed to me that my previous doctors had told him that they didn't expect me to live for the rest of the year after my tumor had been removed.

From my cancer experience, I realized that I'd thought I'd learned all there was to know, that the knowledge I'd received was all too big for me alone, and that I had to give my life away to share it. I was wrong. I just needed to change my perspective. Being sick allowed me to see into my very soul. I saw what I believed, how my belief had played a game with my head, and how my emotions had gotten unmanageable because I felt apart from others. Even though I had no one to talk with. I learned that that really didn't matter. I chose to set boundaries for myself, and to learn to receive as much as I give. It was by far the best decision I ever made. I am far more than a survivor. Now I live life fully. I laugh, and I love, and I feel deeply without covering my feelings up. I don't put things off and over time I have done what I wanted, gone where I wanted to go, and lived as fully as possible. What I got out of the whole cancer and recovery process saved my life.

Today I never know what is next. My guys pop in and out of my awareness, which can frankly be irritating at times. Often, they will come in, commanding me to do something, and I will tell them that I am too busy. They repeat themselves, and I blow them off. If they give their command a third time, I stop, no matter what I am doing, and do whatever they request. Three times is truth no matter what, and I have learned that well. They have never been wrong, and following their directions without question has changed my life dramatically.

I now know that life is magic, and the secrets I'm given aren't mine to keep. I have felt for years as if I've gone to cosmic grad school and have had to find ways here on earth to communicate what I have come to know. The doorways into the cosmos—to the past, present, and future, to unformed reality and the densities we call our world—are very real. If one is paying attention, one can be filled with knowledge that humanity has forgotten. I am no different than you, I've just paid attention. You can too.

My quest to apply what I learned particularly about the pyramids and the universal construct has led me on a personal journey all over the world, where I have visited many so-called sacred sites—some well known, some little known. As I have encountered each, I have begun to recognize that the ancients who came before us left us a complete blueprint of creation, of consciousness, of our history and our destiny. The information contained in these sites is very much the same as what the Masters have shown me. The real secret is that there are no secrets.

The information in this book is a combination of what the Masters have taught me and what I have witnessed within our world as I endeavor to apply to life the amazing things that I have learned. The two are intrinsically and indelibly related. In fact, the information in this book is about life, who we are, and our capabilities. It has always been right in front of us, waiting for interpretation for millennia. The time for us to understand is now, and the translation is resonating infinitely within us, as it always has. As I have traveled the world, encountering what the ancients left behind, I have realized that the Masters brought me a most profound message to give to the world. In my journey, I have come to understand that we truly are the Consciousness within all of Creation.

We are the consciousness within the living One.

Reality isn't happening to us; we are happening to reality. We really do create our experiences, and we can change them at anytime by changing our perceptions.

Over time, science has proven much of the information that my guys have shared over the years. For example, eight months after I published my first book, *Pyramids of Light,* in 2004, the cover of *Science Magazine* included graphics about geometry and creation that were nearly identical to the graphics I had created for my book. The accompanying article matched, in places, nearly word-for-word what I had said in my book, thus proving that what my guys had said, earth's human scientists were saying, too. Scientists are beginning to understand that there is intangible evidence of the existence of unseen worlds. Every day, they are proving what lies beyond the quantum. In laboratories, they are even learning to measure the light emanations of human beings.

Creation is both within us and around us, constantly reinventing itself in every moment. What is infinite has immeasurable facets. It is boundless, and as my guys say, you cannot quantify that which is immeasurable.

From every direction, reality looks a little bit different. Just as each of us looks a little different from the next person, so do our truths. But beyond those perceptions, there is only one truth: that truth that has always been and that, after we are long gone, will always be. The infinite, the ever-changing, ever-regenerating facets of creation are truly timeless.

Matter never dies; it just changes form. Nothing is forever, except for that which is created by us. In that vein, all of the little things don't seem so important anymore. What are important are the messages that we send out to creation every moment that we exist. Our messages to creation bring us the reality we experience, and they affect everything around us, too. It's time we as a whole realize how powerful we are.

Read this book not with skepticism, but with an open mind and a soul that yearns for truth. I think that you will recognize that truth in these pages. As I write these words, a resounding cacophony of voices ring out at once, in a rare moment when all of the Masters speak in unison. The chorus of their voices morphs into threads of glowing streams of light, in a myriad of living colors, that weave together in a tapestry of blinding light.

Aren't we, too, all that?

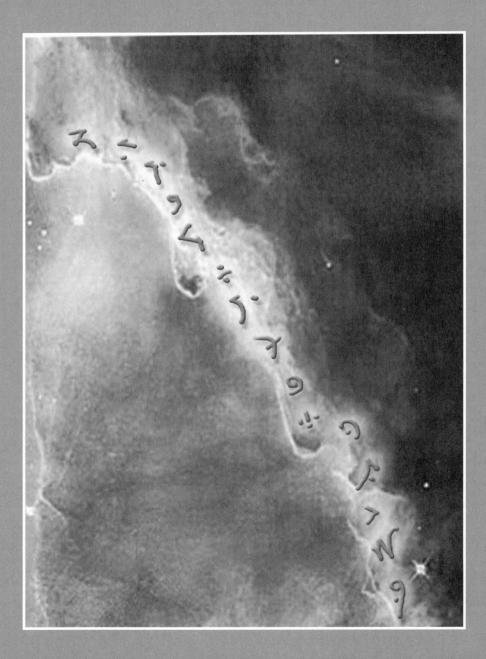

Meditation 1

Letting Go of the Everyday Illusion . . .
Opening to the Infinite

This is the first of eight meditations utilizing ancient symbols. With each of these meditations, your energy field will be initialized to open to different types of higher awareness. You can use these meditations as often as you like or never again, because once you have experienced them, they have become an integral part of your being. There is no particular order for doing these meditations. See what symbol or symbols draw you in, and go within them. Let yourself experience them fully, as if they were old friends.

Imagine yourself opening to the possibility that there are realities beyond your everyday experience that you have not yet been aware of. Imagine that every particle of your being is a door through which you can travel into the unknown. Know that the unknown is nothing to fear and that the experiences that await you are yours because you said, "Yes—I accept."

Chapter Two

Historic Indications of Enlightenment: We Have Been There Before

What we know that we cannot remember is vast compared to the limitations we accept as our current reality.

Both provable history and the oral traditions of nearly all cultures tell us that periods of conscious evolution and expansion have come and gone. In order to understand the phenomenon of changing consciousness, we must first visit at least some of our ancient predecessors.

Interestingly, scientists or archeologists never agree on the truth of some of what has been found. Faced with glaring facts that something greater was going on a long time ago, they demand more proof, more tangible evidence, that there is more to the story than they can envision—and they deny the obvious. The literal brain locks out the memories that are stored in every cell of our beings.

Historically, in every culture on earth, there are a multitude of stories of enlightened beings—people who appear ordinary, but have some sort of connection to the divine. There is also archeological proof that a long time ago there existed technologies that seemed advanced not only for the times they were used in, but even for today. Forged-metal objects and unexplained artifacts have been found in layers of strata millions of years old, long before science accepts that intelligent human beings existed. Evidence of these technologies indicates higher intelligence existed long before human beings supposedly had any real intelligence. Stories abound of gods and goddesses and the relationships between them and human beings.

Stonehenge

Some of the more well-known archeological evidence for periods of high conscious awareness can be found in ancient sacred sites across the globe. Stonehenge is a terrific example. Created of behemoth stones arranged in a circular format, the structure is aligned to multiple astronomical events and the exact cardinal directions. No one knows how the megalithic stones were moved from a quarry far away to their present location. No one knows what the mysterious pattern of the stones means. There have been centuries of speculation, but we don't have a clue. The people who built it did.

The morning I visited Stonehenge for the first time, I felt as if the ancients, with some dry sense of humor, had staged the whole thing. The area was socked with fog, and there was only a hint that anything was out in the field at all. I had my doubts that we would be able to see much. I had arranged for my group to be alone within the site, and anticipation moved my feet closer and closer to the henge.

As I walked up the sidewalk toward the stones, the misty fog parted, and, in all her glory, Stonehenge was revealed. I was awestruck. I felt as if

Stonehenge *(photo by author)*

I had come home. The astronomical relations at Stonehenge are evident; what may not be obvious to many visitors is the sweet energy exchange that happens within the circle. The site is alive, and even though it is damaged, with some stones missing and others broken, the inbuilt harmonics are still at play today. Although its original purpose is a mystery, Stonehenge remains a powerful place of healing and energy exchange.

· *The Pyramids*

We cannot explore historic references to enlightenment without mentioning the pyramids of ancient Egypt and Teotihuacan. They stand as reminders of the basic format of all reality. They are representative of a specific sacred, geometrical format that is a complete set of universal truths. These truths indicate the basic construct of all matter and the organization of reality.

Majestically rising above the earth is the site of Teotihuacan, in Mexico. The Pyramids of the Sun and the Moon, as well as the Pyramid of Quetzalcoatl, defy the ravages of time. No one remembers who built the pyramids there. The site has been occupied by multiple cultures. Finding the site vacated, the ancient Toltec people occupied the site and lived there in peace. The Toltec women were held in high esteem, and special quarters were built for their activities of healing, birthing, ceremony, and wisdom gathering.

The Toltec Eagle Knights were the highest echelon of the culture. They intuited everything about everything, from how to build the temples and lay out the temple site, to details about everyday living and the relativity of celestial events. The Eagle Knights were much like gods on earth, directing the Toltec society and its people by using information they brought back from the ethers. In the Temple of the Butterfly, the Eagle Knights gazed into a celestial pool of water that was lined with obsidian. There, they read the movements of the stars as a celestial instruction manual for life on earth. Even today, paintings remaining in the Jaguar Temple, where the Eagle Knights communicated with other dimensions, can take the seeker of spirit into other worlds. In a separate temple were the knights' sleeping quarters. There, other surviving paintings take the willing experiencer into other times and places and even into ancient Teotihuacan itself. Throughout the temple site are several more interdimensional portals. Once one enters the room with the portal, spirit guides come forth to take the experiencer into transdimensional journeys, or they bring messages for the willing listener.

A second vitally important group within the Toltec society was the Jaguar Warriors. These brave men stalked not only their enemies, but also each other—and themselves. They learned every intricacy of their own beings—their motivations, their perceptions, and their beliefs, dissecting them for greater awareness of their inner and outer worlds. The Jaguar Warriors were hypervigilant in every way imaginable.

The Toltec culture was one of peaceful coexistence with the earth, of symbiosis with the land, the water, and the stars. But like the Anasazi, the Mayans, and others, they simply vanished. To this day, no one knows for sure where they went.

The Aztec people found the Teotihuacan site abandoned. They fled to the pyramids of Teotihuacan when the Spaniards ravaged their original utopia, which is now Mexico City.

Teotihuacan is like no other place on the planet. The energy flows so intensely there that it can be literally disorienting. The first time I climbed up the Pyramid of the Sun and sat at the exact center of the apex, I could feel a huge current of energy flowing. Ultimately I became so disoriented that someone had to show me the way down.

The angles and measurements of the Teotihuacan pyramids share uncanny similarities with those of the pyramids halfway across the world in Egypt. The pyramids in Egypt are believed to have been constructed as tombs for the elite—for pharaohs and their entourages. But they are not just tombs—they are roadmaps. Just like the pyramids the Masters showed me, the pyramids of Egypt are complete maps to the form of creation beyond the quantum and into the infinite. The pyramids in both Egypt and Teotihuacan are considered by many to open and expand access to levels of consciousness more so than other, less-powerful energy centers in the world. Both sets of pyramids are aligned to mirror part of the star constellation of Orion, specifically Orion's belt.

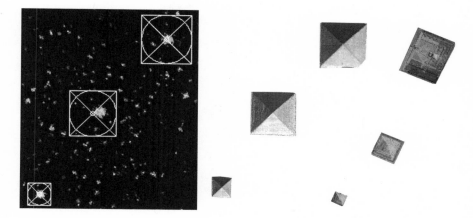

Left, the alignment of Orion's belt. Middle, the alignment of the pyramids at Giza in Egypt. Right, the alignment of the pyramids in Teotihuacan.

Each of the pyramids has interior chambers in which specific sets of harmonics occur. If one were to measure these internal harmonics, one would find that those within each pyramid innately emit overtones of sound that resonate at different frequencies. From the step pyramids in the Yucatan to the mammoth pyramids at Giza, each site has a slightly different set of internal harmonics.

Yet each pyramid site is also harmonically relative. They have a specific harmonic relationship with each other, and each also has a specific harmonic relationship with the earth, the ley lines, and the cosmos. You might say that by virtue of their very existence, the pyramids across the world create an infinite symphony of harmonics, with overtones that reach across dimensions and into the infinite.

Varying styles and sizes of pyramids can be found not only in Egypt and Teotihuacan, but also at predictable measurable increments of longitude and latitude all over the earth. The relative locations of pyramids and other sacred sites around the globe lead to speculation that ancient people were working to construct a worldwide grid of sacred sites that were relative not only to harmonics, but also to levels of or access points to consciousness. The pyramids not only occupy specific places, but they also seem to have harmonic purpose for the planet and its inhabitants.

Many—in fact, most—of the pyramids that we see today were built by people for whom we have no written history. Yet obviously these people existed. Archeologists and other scientists have created a vast range of supposition as to the purpose of the pyramids. Having experienced many of them personally, I maintain that the pyramids are living examples of creation and consciousness in its most basic format. This format includes harmonic sets of frequencies that under certain conditions become not only active, but also interactive, universally, interdimensionally, and therefore to some degree in our third-dimensional reality as well. The four-sided pyramid is the building block of all creation.

It is no coincidence that the pyramid alignments often replicate the alignments of the star constellations of Orion's belt and the Pleiades. Nor is it coincidence that other sacred sites are built on ley-line convergences, aligning to specific astronomical events with unerring accuracy. These artifacts from times lost are entirely indicative of periods of higher awareness, consciousnesss, and intelligence.

The Sumerians and the Story of Gilgamesh

The ancient Sumerians left behind remarkable proof of higher awareness. They have provided us with a series of carved stone tablets depicting the idea of accessing greater conscious awareness and even the benefits of doing so. The tablets describe the prediluvian story of Gilgamesh. The text is written in poetic form and tells an engaging story of a time and place we can only imagine. The story opens with the main character, Gilgamesh, realizing his own enlightenment as he is taught by Anu in the methodology of the old mystery schools: giving adepts a first-hand experience of higher consciousness.

TABLET I

He who has seen everything, *I will make known* (?) to the lands.
I will teach (?) about him who experienced all things,
        . . . alike,
Anu granted him the totality of knowledge of *all*.
He saw the Secret, discovered the Hidden,

he brought information of (the time) before the Flood.
He went on a distant journey, pushing himself to
    exhaustion,
but then was brought to peace.
He carved on a stone stela all of his toils,
and built the wall of Uruk-Haven,
the wall of the sacred Eanna Temple, the holy sanctuary.
Look at its wall which gleams like *copper* (?),
inspect its inner wall, the likes of which no one can equal!
Take hold of the threshold stone—it dates from ancient times!
Go close to the Eanna Temple, the residence of Ishtar,
such as no later king or man ever equaled!
    Go up on the wall of Uruk and walk around,
examine its foundation, inspect its brickwork thoroughly.
Is not (even the core of) the brick structure made of kiln-fired brick,
and did not the Seven Sages themselves lay out its plans?
One league city, one league palm gardens, one league lowlands, the
    open area (?) of the Ishtar Temple,
three leagues and the open area (?) of Uruk it (the wall) encloses.
Find the copper tablet box,
open the . . . of its lock of bronze,
undo the fastening of its secret opening.
Take and read out from the lapis lazuli tablet
how Gilgamesh went through every hardship.
Supreme over other kings, lordly in appearance,
he is the hero, born of Uruk, the goring wild bull.
He walks out in front, the leader,
and walks at the rear, trusted by his companions.
Mighty net, protector of his people,
raging flood-wave who destroys even walls of stone!
Offspring of Lugalbanda, Gilgamesh is strong to perfection,
son of the august cow, Rimat-Ninsun; . . . Gilgamesh is
    awesome to perfection.
It was he who opened the mountain passes,
who dug wells on the flank of the mountain.
It was he who crossed the ocean, the vast seas, to the
    rising sun,

who explored the world regions, seeking life.
It was he who reached by his own sheer strength Utanapishtim, the
    Faraway,
who restored the sanctuaries (or: cities) that the Flood had
    destroyed!
. . . for teeming mankind.
Who can compare with him in kingliness?
Who can say like Gilgamesh: "I am King!"?
Whose name, from the day of his birth, was called "Gilgamesh"?
Two-thirds of him is god, one-third of him is human.
The Great Goddess [Aruru] designed (?) the model for his body,
she prepared his form
. . . beautiful, handsomest of men,
. . . perfect

• • •

Because he has experienced altered realms of consciousness, Gilgamesh realizes that he is more than mere mortal. Because he has realized a higher state of awareness and, therefore, is no longer subject to the limitations of earthly realities and illusions, he accepts his perfection. He loses the sense that he is imperfect in any way. Because Gilgamesh no longer sees himself as limited, others believe him to be unlimited as well. Public perception of him is reflected in the references that he is a king and two-thirds God. The reason he is only two-thirds God is that one part of him remains in human form, dense matter and experiential, emotional, and somewhat with an ego. As long as he is any part human, he is only part God.

The important aspect of the story of Gilgamesh is his ability to reach beyond his human mind and into the ethers for greater realizations. He is a prime example of humanity seeking its divinity and marrying the two in everyday life.

Ancient Astronomy and Technology: Prophecy or Historical Records?

In order to experience any level of reality, one must first have the awareness that reality is even possible. Awareness can be thought of as the

An ancient Sumerian carving depicting the pathway of an asteroid that collided with the earth, destroying the cities of Sodom and Gomorrah. (Kuyunjik Collection, British Museum, London)

beginning of the heightening of consciousness. Many ancient cultures left behind evidence of technologies far more advanced than what we have even today; they could not have created and used those technologies without some kind of heightened awareness.

There is an old story of a medicine man, an indigenous shaman, who walked to the edge of land and looked across the ocean. Lo and behold, he saw a fleet of ships—something that had never been witnessed by him or his people. Inherently, the shaman sensed that the ships were a threat to his people. He sent out an alarm, and the people of the tribe came running to meet him at the water's edge. But when they arrived, none of them could see the ships. Because the ships were not part of their conceivable reality, the people had no frame of reference for such a vastly different actuality. They had never seen a ship or even knew that one might exist. The shaman could see the ships because he was able and willing to consider the extended possibilities of reality beyond the known. Once the people were made aware of the ships, they began to see them.

What we are not aware of we cannot conceive of. The evidence that we have from archeology alone proves that ancient people not only were aware of, but also conceived, created, and utilized amazing forms of measurement, technology, architecture, and more.

In addition to the story of Gilgamesh, according to a press release issued March 31, 2008 by the University of Bristol in the United Kingdom, the Sumerians left a written record of an asteroid collision with the earth. This record is in the form of a clay tablet, referred to as the Planisphere. It puzzled scientists for 150 years and has recently been identified as a witness's account of the asteroid suspected of being the destructive force behind the devastation of the cities of Sodom and Gomorrah. Researchers who cracked the code of the cuneiform symbols on the Planisphere tablet are convinced that its carvings depict the flight and descending path of an asteroid that is believed to have been more than half a mile across.

The tablet, found by Henry Layard in the remains of the library in the royal palace at Nineveh in the mid-19th century, is thought to be a 700 BC copy of notes made by a Sumerian astronomer who was watching the night sky. The astronomer referred to the asteroid as "white stone bowl approaching" and noted its movement as it "vigorously swept along." Using computers to re-create the night sky thousands of years ago, scientists have pinpointed the astronomer's sighting to shortly before dawn on June 29 in the year 3123 BC. Since the asteroid was hollow, it did not leave a crater in the ground.

In order to have knowledge of astronomy and the relationship of foreign objects moving in a destructive path within the solar system, one would first have to have awareness that the possibility exists.

Ancient Egypt

One of the first experiences I had when working from a state of higher consciousness was the realization that consciousness, in its truest form, is spherical in shape. When one is in an enlightened state, the consciousness expands and literally radiates outward from the body. As it does, other people are attracted to the energy, but often mistakenly believe that the person who is radiating the expanded energy is special in some way.

Isis (photo courtesy of Van Villanti)

From my personal experience, as well as the teachings of ancient cultures, I know that individual consciousness can be merged with the infinite consciousness, which is the universal mind. It can also be intentionally merged with the energy field of another person for the purpose of healing or teaching via pure energy. In fact, we can literally hold consciousness in our hands.

Representations of spherical consciousness are clearly demonstrated in ancient Egyptian temples, burial chambers, and hieroglyphs. The ancient Egyptians depicted orbs of light as being carried over the heads of lines of men and over the heads of individual god or goddess entities. For example, the goddess Isis is pictured with a red orb above her head. An orb and its placement above a figure's head are recognizable worldwide, even in current times, as symbolizing the figure's higher consciousness.

In different locations and in reference to different deities, the spheres of consciousness are shown in both red and yellow. The difference in color indicates different frequencies of origin and consciousness. The red orbs are representative of Mars energy, which entered the earth's awareness in what is often referred to as "the before times," past times that are far beyond our remembering or recorded history. The ancient Egyptians had at least some awareness of the harmonics of Mars and applied them as acceptable aspects of higher knowing. The energy of the frequencies of consciousness on Mars is very different from the energy of the frequencies of consciousness on Earth. It is a much heavier and more intense than the earthly yellow energy, which is very high frequency and less dense.

Maat (photo courtesy of luminati.net)

Another terrific example of enlightenment depicted in orb form in ancient Egypt is that of the god Ptah, who was a creator deity. The image was found in the tomb of Ramesses III. From the yellow color of his symbol of enlightenment, one can assume that Ptah actually came into his enlightenment from an original human perspective. In other words, he learned to open his consciousness to higher awareness.

Another depiction of enlightenment comes from the tomb of Twosret. It depicts Maat, the goddess of truth, justice, and order, with a particularly beautiful orb of consciousness. The orb's red center is surrounded by an outer edge of yellow energy. The orb does not seem to need any external support, which indicates that Maat was more advanced in her conscious nature and likely extremely mysterious to everyday people. Maat not only carried infinite aspects of consciousness, but she also embodied consciousness. This blending of her earthly and divine selves made her a true goddess.

Ancient Egyptians didn't just respect higher awareness; they also used it. They knew how to create electrical-current flow in the form of a crude battery. They understood alchemy and made monatomic gold, which was baked into the bread of pharaohs and priests. The gold, when ingested, was believed to create enlightenment and access to higher realms. Despite an apparent lack of technology, the Egyptians moved rocks that weighed several tons. They understood that there were veils, thin barriers, between the worlds of the living and the dead, gods and humans. Further, the ancient Egyptians spoke with other-worldly beings that they believed to be gods. They interacted with other interdimensional creatures, which assisted them in transforming from

Light bulb at Dendera (photo © 2006 Alf Kontermann, use granted under CCA SA 2.5)

human form to light bodies and showed the Egyptians the way to other worlds after death.

Clear evidence of ancient Egyptian technology and higher awareness is shown on a spectacular carved panel that hangs inside the entrance to Abydos, a temple dedicated to Osiris. The panel, situated just below the ceiling, clearly depicts aircraft such as a helicopter, a space shuttle, a glider, and missiles, as well as some other, unknown technology. Egyptologists would like us to think that the panel is prophesying modern technology, because otherwise they would have to admit that the panel indicates the Egyptians actually *did* have such advanced technology. Whether you believe that the panel is prophesying today's technology or showing off ancient technology, the question remains: *how did the ancient Egyptians know about these things?*

In contrast to what the Egyptologists say, Masters such as Osiris, from the unseen dimensions clearly indicate that this series of panels is telling the story of Atlantis. Atlantis is purported to have been destroyed by weapons similar to those depicted in the panels. Some people have suggested that the ancient Egyptians placed this panel at Abydos as a warning to future generations of the destructive power of weaponry. This seems likely,

Closeup of the panel inside the entrance to Abydos (photo courtesy of luminati.net)

considering that several images show technology that we do not possess, such as the domed, UFO-looking objects or the object to the left of helicopter, which is possibly a rocket-type ship but more closely resembles a submarine.

It is my contention that some of these craft are actually Vimana, aircraft flown by the ancient Indian people. (I'll talk more about the Vimana in a few pages.)

Another example of the ancients' knowledge of "modern" technology can be found at Dendera, a temple dedicated to Hathor. There, an absolutely startling stone panel reveals that the ancients knew about DNA. The panel shows two men holding a sealed glass container that has a double helix (DNA) inside. Even more stunning is another huge Dendera panel showing what is unmistakably a humongous light bulb. The light bulb appears to be connected by some sort of a wire to a power source.

The power source may have been a variation of what is known as the Baghdad Battery. Several such "batteries" were unearthed near Baghdad, Iraq, in the mid-1930s. They consist of five-inch-high terracotta jars, each containing a copper cylinder with an iron rod inserted into it. When the pots were filled with an acidic juice, such as lemon juice, grape juice, or even vinegar, the liquid surrounded the cylinder and rod, causing elec-

Panel at Dendera, showing DNA strand (photo courtesy of luminati.net)

trophoresis, or electrically induced particle movement. The power generated by the jars may have been used for electroplating jewelry, as well as powering various other technologies.

Egypt alone offers vast evidence of ancient technologies and previous periods of higher awareness, but there is more such proof all over the planet.

Other Visual Depictions of Higher Consciousness

Illustrations of expanded consciousness appear not only in ancient Egyptian art, but also in petroglyphs and pictographs on rocks around the world. One beautiful and clear example can be found at the visitor's center at the Ginko Petrified Forest State Park just outside of Vantage, Washington. The petroglyph depicts a person or being with rays of light that form a spherical kind of halo circling his head.

Other artistic representations of individuals with access to higher consciousness show a halo, flat disk, or glow from the person's head, instead of a sphere above the head. Such radiant halos can be seen in paintings of Jesus, his mother Mary, and the saints, as well as other persons deemed to be holy.

Interestingly, the spheres, halos, and glows above the head of the subjects are not used for large groups of people but only for individuals. For example, in a single painting, Jesus, Mary, and John the Baptist may all

Petroglyph at Ginko Petrified Forest in Washington State (photo courtesy of D.L. Anderson)

Jesus with a halo

have halos, but the crowds listening to Jesus speak do not, even though, through his teachings, they are being enlightened to at least some degree. It would appear that the spheres, halos, and other indicators of spiritual enlightenment (which is also expansion of consciousness) are reserved for those who stand out of the crowd, so to speak, using their knowledge and awareness for teachings of a higher nature.

Ancient Flying Machines of India and Tibet

In ancient India, the emperor Ashoka put together a secret committee of India's greatest scientists. He called the group the "Secret Society of the Nine Unknown Men." It was the job of the society to catalogue all of their secret sciences. Ashoka was afraid that if these sciences were discovered by the wrong people, they could be used for evil purposes in war. The group wrote a series of nine books, one of which was about antigravity technology.

Several Sanskrit documents, discovered by the Chinese in Lhasa, Tibet, also contain references to antigravity technology. Translated by Dr. Ruth Reyna of the University of Chandrigarh, these documents give directions for constructing interstellar spaceships that are propelled by a "centrifugal force strong enough to counteract all gravitational pull." Reyna said that this method of propulsion was based upon "laghima," an unknown power of the ego that exists in man's physiological makeup. This is the same laghima that Hindu yogis say causes a person to levitate. This force, as we will discover later, utilizes the actual particles that comprise the construct of creation in order to bridge matter and energy within the universal construct, thereby defying gravity. According to Dr. Reyna, with these flying machines, called "astras" in the ancient texts, detachments of men could be sent to any planet.

The documents containing the information about the astras are said to be many thousands of years old. They also purportedly contain the secrets of "antima," or a cap of invisibility, and "garima," or the ability to become heavy as a mountain of lead (the complete opposite of laghima, a simple reversing of particulate polarities).

These aircraft that the Indian people apparently built and used to fly all over the world were called Vimana. There were apparently four types, all of which very much resemble UFOs that have been reportedly sighted all over the planet. One type was a double-decker, saucer-shaped craft that had portal windows and a dome. This craft was said to move at the speed of the wind and make a melodious sound. Another type of Vimana was a cigar-shaped craft.

According to some of the ancient texts, the Vimana took off vertically and could not only fly, but also hover, like a helicopter or a blimp. They could switch from a free energy source of power to solar power.

In addition to the texts that give full instructions for constructing the Vimana, there are others giving flight instructions and precautions. In fact, there are so many texts referring to the Vimana that they would fill countless books.

What if the ancient Indian people not only built aircraft that flew and could travel in outer space, but also built craft that were able to cross the space-time continuum? What if some of the aircraft we see and report as UFOs were nothing more than ancient Vimana flitting in and out of our space and time?

The Dogon

The Dogon people, who live in the central plateau region of the African country of Mali, have a mysterious heritage that seems to extend back to a period of enlightenment predating written history. Allegedly, when the Dogon left Egypt, they brought to their new lands sacred knowledge in the form of oral traditions, which were perhaps handed down to them by the ancient priests of Egypt.

The Dogon creation tale is laced with metaphors similar to those of other legends throughout the world, such as the ancient Egyptian tales of Isis, Horus, and Osirus, and the Christian stories of Jesus, Mary, and Joseph. They also resemble the stories of many South American tribes and even those of the indigenous people of North America. One need only compare these stories and their metaphoric content to understand that the nature of our reality—past, present, and future—is interlinked in universal consciousness and filters down to human experience over eons.

According to Dogon mythology, Nommo was the first living being created by Amma, the sky god and creator of the universe. Nommo soon multiplied to become six pairs of twins. (Twins are a metaphor for the one source/soul splitting into two parts—yin and yang—when it enters the electromagnetic energies of third dimension. The six pairs of twins also represent the twelve-strand structure of DNA, the initial genetic instructions for the Dogon.) One twin rebelled against the order established by Amma, thereby destabilizing the universe. (This story is also reminiscent of the Old Testament story of Cain and Abel. The focus on our duality has always been to maintain and restore balance between the light and dark so that we will be ready for Judgment Day.)

In order to purify the cosmos and restore its order, Amma sacrificed one of the Nommo twins, whose body was cut up and scattered throughout the universe. The distribution of the parts of the Nommo's body is seen as a metaphor for the proliferation of Binu shrines throughout the Dogon region. It is believed that the Binu shrines accommodate the spirits of mythic ancestors who lived in the times before mankind began to experience death.

This story is eerily similar to the Egyptian story of Isis, Osiris, and Horus. Osiris was said to rise from the dead as the savior of his people and as a symbol of light. The Nommo story is also similar to the biblical tale of the last supper Jesus' disciples shared with him before he was captured by the Romans. During the meal, Jesus told them, "Take this bread and eat it, for it is my body. Take this wine and drink it for it is my blood." Jesus later rose from the dead as a symbol of light in the world.

The ancient Dogon had a clear understanding of science and mathematics that was light years ahead of what other evolved people on the earth had at that time. For instance, the Dogon used binary numbers to depict their origins.

However, the nature and source of some of the Dogon's scientific information has been considered controversial. From 1931 to 1956, Marcel Griaule and Germaine Dieterlen, French archeologists, spent twenty-five years embedded with the Dogon, during which time they were initiated into the tribe. Griaule and Dieterlen found that the Dogon appeared to know that the brightest star in the sky, Sirius, has a barely visible companion, Sirius B, which can only be seen with a high-powered telescope. The Dogon also knew about the rings around Saturn, and the multiple moons of Jupiter, which were not discovered by astronomers until after the invention of the telescope in the 17th century. Obviously, no telescopes were available to the Dogon people.

The controversy worsened when author Robert Temple proposed that there was an extra-terrestrial source of the Dogon's celestial knowledge. Sadly, if they knew anything about the source of the Dogon's celestial knowledge, Griaule and Dieterlen never divulged the information.

• • •

There are more examples of historic evidence that can prove, time and again, that periods of expanded consciousness have existed throughout earth's history. The point is that sometimes, in the name of science, obvious clues to our origins and abilities are denied or overlooked. Science dismisses or ignores these clues because even though the infinite is accessible, it is not clearly definable or measurable.

Civilizations Beyond Provable History

Outside of provable history are prevailing tales of civilizations that have come and gone. One cannot know for sure the actual facts that may have existed beyond our historical records. On the other hand, that the stories linger and are, in many cases, consistent in form, with perhaps only small details being altered from one teller to the next, leads us to take a second look and to wonder. After all, in every tale there is or was some grain of truth. Whether the stories are brought forward orally or by cellular memory, they bear consideration.

Further, many, many people who have honed their intuitive nature and are able to access realities outside of the limited human perspective have had nearly identical visions and experiences of these mythical worlds. Some even have past-life memories of these places, and those memories contain a myriad of details.

Since we are exploring aspects of consciousness and the possibility that more advanced consciousness was prevalent at times in history, it would be remiss to not address these mythical civilizations.

Lemuria

The ancient civilization of Lemuria, or Mu, as it is sometimes called, apparently existed off the current coasts of Central and South America. Much of the Lemurian culture was located in Peru and later in Guatemala, Bolivia, and Mexico. It is said to have been an expanded settlement that reached across to the South Pacific and perhaps as far as Japan. (Current archeological questions address a possible pyramid that has been found underwater on the coast of Japan, along with potentially manmade artifacts.)

The Lumurian people were light beings, not having solid, physical structure. They were originally psychic projections of reality from across dimensions. Eventually, as the Lemurians remained on the earth plane, their bodies began to become denser, taking at first nebulous forms and later becoming solid matter in the form of physical bodies. But they retained access to the infinite consciousness that they had had when they first entered the earth environment.

The Lemurians were not "space men"; they were other-dimensional beings—beings that lived at frequencies of reality that are very different than ours. Because they were such beings and because they were able to travel transdimensionally, they were able to change the form of matter from its most dense state to its least dense state, which is not affected by gravity. They performed the change by altering the actual electromagnetic field of the subject or object. They applied this transformation process to their bodies, as well as using it to change the form of rock in relation to gravity, for instance. By interrupting the construct of harmonics within an area of the earthly plane, the Lemurians moved solid stone to construct a livable environment during their stay within the earth plane. Some of their technology was passed down to the Atlanteans and, later, to the ancient Egyptians.

The Lemurians were a very intelligent group of beings, with little access to emotions and definite black-and-white perceptions. They utilized sacred geometric formats in all of their structural designs. Their buildings were constructed to amplify energy and also to stabilize it.

An excellent example of Lemurian construction still exists in Tiahuanaco, a major sacred ceremonial center and archeological site in the highlands of Bolivia. Tiahuanaco is laid out in a form that is identical to the star constellation Pleiades. The site is also aligned with major astronomical events.

There, a stone pyramid known as the Akapana was found covered in sand. Much of the site is yet to be excavated, but what has been explored has revealed anomalous structures and displays a command of electromagnetic energy that we have yet to fully comprehend. Atop the main pyramid are two rows of columnar stone. Although to the naked eye this stone appears to be nothing more than rock of some kind, it is in fact magnetic. When one holds a compass up to any of these stones, each shows a different north. The energy of these stones is so immense that one can actually feel it when placing their hands or body against them.

Standing atop the pyramid structure, I had the sense of being pulled down toward its center. There appeared to be further energy anomalies down inside of the pyramid. One gets the feeling that there is a lot yet to be excavated that is relative to the magnetic columns above.

When I took a group to Tiahuanaco recently, several of us actually became uncomfortable from the buildup of energy in our bodies. Each of us experienced the sensation of warped energy flow, and it was as if the energy of the site was out of tune within our bodies. The feeling of the energy anomaly ran from the left ribcage across our backs and down to the right kidney area. The sensation became more intense the longer we were there.

When the Spaniards discovered this site during their rampage of Central and South Americas, they toppled many of its stones and structures, knocking the electromagnetic energy grid out of harmony. The well-known Sun Gate is not in its original place within the site. No one really knows where it belongs, and to anyone who is energy sensitive, the feeling of incongruence of energy is obvious when standing near it.

Also on the site is a small temple that is below ground level. This temple displays an amazing array of carved stone heads that appear to be from most every race of people on the earth. In addition to these carvings, each panel of faces displays a white stone carved face that look to be alien in nature. There is a discernable difference between the race faces and the white carved ones.

Precisely carved and paid stone gateway at Tiahuanaco (photo by author)

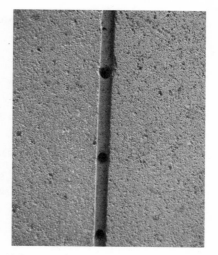

Star map on right shoulder of central statue at Puma Punka (photo by author)

A 6 mm, perfectly cut groove, with equidistant drill holes inside the groove (photo by author)

In the central area of Tiahuanaco there stands a male figure with carvings all over his body. His hands hold two different objects, one of which looks like a vault or box with a key in the top. His fingers are carved as if he has two left hands, except that his right thumb is placed appropriately. This silent guardian holds a yet-undiscovered message for those who visit the site. Most interesting about this statue is the apparent star map on his right shoulder. On the map are vector lines that seem to point to a certain destination in the stars.

One gets the sense that there is much more than meets the eye at Tiahuanaco, and that if it were repaired and the electromagnetic fields reestablished, an interdimensional grid would spring back to life. Personally, I would love to take a multi-discipline group of scientists to study the energy anomalies there.

Arthur Posnansky, a German-Bolivian scholar, exhaustively studied Tiahuanaka for nearly fifty years. While he lived at the ruins, he became intimately familiar with them and noticed scores of anomalies that didn't fit normal archeological guidelines or the chronological framework of the site. For example, strewn across the site were massive blocks of stone that no known pre-Columbian culture supposedly had the know-how to carve or transport.

Even more astounding, the spatial arrangement of the structures (their relationship to each another and to the stars above) suggested that the initial site engineers had a highly complex knowledge of astronomy, geomancy, and mathematics.

Not far from Puma Punka and the Akapana pyramid are the Kalasasaya compound and the ostensible subterranean temple. It was here that Posnansky discovered the anomalies that led him to propose not only a great antiquity for Tiahuanaco but also an extraordinary use. In his endeavors to comprehend the site, Posnansky conducted exact surveys of all of the main structures of Tiahuanaco. The Kalasasaya structure, a rectangular enclosure that measured 450 feet by 400 feet, was outlined by a series of vertical stone pillars (the name Kalasasaya means "the standing pillars") that were oriented east to west. Using his measurements of the lines of sight along these stone pillars, the orientation of the Kalasasaya, and the apparently intentional departures from the cardinal points, Posnansky showed that the alignment of the construction was based upon an astronomical principle called "the obliquity of the ecliptic."

This term, the obliquity of the ecliptic, refers to the angle between the plane of the earth's orbit and that of the celestial equator. This angle is currently equal to approximately 23 degrees and 27 minutes. In its natural progression, the tilt of the obliquity changes slowly, bit by bit over long periods of time. Its cyclic variation ranges between 22 degrees, 1 minute and 24 degrees, 5 minutes over a period of 41,000 years. This works out to about 1 degree in 7,000 years.

This cycle isn't the same as the precessional cycle of 25,920 years or 1 degree of movement every 72 years that we find in the Mayan calendar. Posnansky calculated that the obliquity of the ecliptic at the time the Kalasasaya was built was 23 degrees, 8 minutes, and 48 seconds. Based on these computations, Posnansky was able to date the original construction of the Kalasasaya and Tiahuanaco at about 15,000 BC. This date was later validated by a team of four prestigious astronomers from multiple universities in Germany.

Posnansky's new date was much older than was even considered possible by the existing paradigm of human history and has since continuously been ridiculed by mainstream archaeologists and pre-historians. But it is not so easy to let go of Posnansky's findings because more mysteries abound in Tiahuanaco that seem to confirm far ancient beginnings of the site. Some of these mysteries arise from all over the Andean region as ancient myths of Tiahuanaco. The stories tell about its origin and use in a pre-flood time. Scientific studies prove that a cataclysmic flood actually did occur around 12,000 years ago. Further, the utensils, tools, and fragments of human skeletons found embedded in the deepest layers of the flood alluvia show that the site was used pre-flood. Also found across the site were detailed, mysterious carvings of bearded, non-Andean people, which are completely unique in the western hemisphere.

Writers such as Graham Hancock, Zecharia Sitchin, and Ivar Zapp have suggested that Posnansky's data strongly suggests that the original Tiahuanaco civilization successfully existed more than a few thousand years before the period of time that has been assumed by conventional archaeologists.

Rather than rising and falling during the two millennia around the time of Christ as first thought, Tiahuanaco likely existed during the last Ice Age, at least 15,000 to 20,000 years ago. What this suggests is remarkable: *Tiahuanaco may be a fragment of a civilization that may have included sites such as Teotihuacan in Mexico, Baalbek in Lebanon, and the Great Pyramid in Egypt.*

Also in Bolivia, at nearby Puma Punka, precision-cut stones weighing over 100 tons litter the earth. Local guides will tell you that perhaps Puma Punka was once a port of a then much larger Lake Titicaca. Nothing there appeared to be a port of any kind. It is as if a great shaking event loosed the stones of the structures there, devastating the city. On this fascinating archeological site are monolithic stones of granite or diorite that are etched or carved with lines and drill marks. Because diorite is one of the hardest known types of rock on earth, the *only* way that these cuts could been made was with either a diamond-tipped drill and blades or a laser of some sort. The stones were cut in "H" shapes in order to be interlocking. The precision of the cut of the stones, along with the degree of polish that remains on many of the stone blocks today, negates any possibility that they were created by primitive people. When one touches the stones it is surprising to feel not only their smoothness, but the literal sensation of softness—even though to the naked eye they appear to be rough.

In Puma Punka, certain chambers within the now-toppled structures may have held and amplified subtle energies for what the Lemurians called regeneration. In order for their light bodies to remain in balance on the earth plane, occasionally the Lemurians' subtle energy fields had to be attuned. Within these chamber walls, sets of pure harmonics were emitted, which in turn realigned the particulates of the form of matter that was reflected as the Lemurian body. It was this same light form that the Lemurians were able to alter for interdimensional travel. Even today, the perfect balance of energy can be felt at Puma Punka. Ancient Egyptians built replicas of these chambers in some of their temples. These chambers were utilized as mystery schools.

The Lemurians saw prehistoric humans as a means of populating their workforces. They interbred with early humans to create beings to use as slave labor, thereby becoming one of the five main root races that contributed to the gene pool of evolving humanity. When the Lemurians left the earth plane, their descendants evolved through further interbreeding with developing humans and inevitably into the dense mass of human being.

Today, those of Lemurian descent are generally tall, with very defined and angulated bone structure. They have light body hair and pale complexions. Generally their hair is very straight and can vary in color, and it may tend toward premature graying. Lemurian descendants are very practical people with dry senses of humor. They are often brilliant and tend to be more interested in the sciences than more esoteric subjects. Even though they may appear to be left-brain oriented, they may have a flair for spontaneity and drama.

Other potential evidence of Lemurian existence are crystal skulls that have been found in South America. The shapes and smoothness of these skulls can only be the result of extremely advanced shaping and polishing techniques. The skulls are said to demonstrate metaphysical properties, such as seeming to be lit from within when no apparent

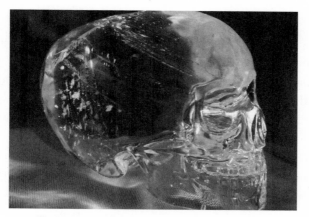
The Mitchell-Hedges crystal skull (photo by Alice Bryant)

outside light source is present, enabling spontaneous healing, and emitting voices and tones. The technology required to create such exquisite artistry is rare, if it is found at all in the world today. Harmonic frequencies could have been utilized to rearrange the form of the crystal in order to shape it. This process would have generated a great deal of heat as the particles of the crystal became excited, malleable, and reorganized.

Some suspect that these crystal skulls originated in Atlantis, but this is not likely the case, as their properties appear to be more of an interdimensional nature.

The Lemurians were particularly interested in certain rock formations, which contained ores that they mined. The ore was utilized in alchemic processes. The offspring of their interbreeding with humans were utilized as slaves for the mining endeavors.

There came a time during the Lemurian occupation of Earth when great quakes began to occur. The earth's crust shook violently, and lava began to flow freely across the land. Geologically, right before an earthquake, bursts of electromagnetic energy are released from within the earth. The environment became so unstable and the electromagnetic releases from the earth so intense that the Lemurians were unable to maintain balance in this earth plane. They evacuated their settlements and returned to their home dimensions, leaving their denser, human cohorts, as well as their mixed-race descendants, behind.

The Atlanteans

Atlantis is one of, if not *the,* most enigmatic mythical cultures in the world. Stories abound about this great mythical society. The great mystery of Atlantis's predemise location haunts searchers even today. If any of the myths about Atlantis are true, this society can prove to be the perfect example of a civilization of people with great awareness and access to higher consciousness.

The first recorded story of the lost continent of Atlantis comes from 355 BC and the Greek philosopher Plato. In his writings, Plato used dialogues to express his ideas. In one of his dialogues, his ideas were explored in a series of arguments and debates between characters of story. Plato often used real people, such as his teacher, Socrates, to personify his own ideas.

In Plato's book *Timaeus,* a character named Kritias gives an account of Atlantis that had been passed down in his family for generations. According to Kritias, the story was originally told by a priest to Kritias's ancestor Solon when Solon visited Egypt. The story goes that there had been a prevailing empire located to the west of the "pillars of Hercules" (what is now known as the Strait of Gibraltar), on an island in the Atlantic Ocean. The civilization there had been established by Poseidon, the god of the sea. Poseidon fathered five sets of twins on the island. (Sound familiar? Remember the Dogons?) The continent and surrounding area was named for Poseidon's firstborn son, Atlas. Poseidon divided the land into ten sectors, each of which was to be ruled by a son or the son's heirs.

The capital city of Atlantis was a wonder of architecture and engineering. The city was laid out in a series of concentric walls and canals. At the very center of the layout was a hill. On top of the hill was a temple dedicated to Poseidon. Inside the temple was a gold statue of Poseidon driving six winged horses.

According to Plato's *Timaeus,* about nine thousand years before the time of Plato, the people of Atlantis became corrupt and greedy, and the gods decided to destroy them. A violent earthquake shook the land, giant waves rolled over the shores, and the island sank into the sea, never to be seen again.

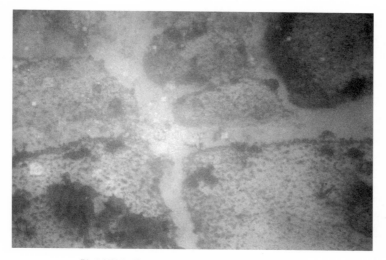

Bimini Wall off Bimini Island (photo © Michael Tierney)

Speculation by scholars, historians, scientists, psychics, and others has placed Atlantis in a number of locations, but so far, though, no accepted, concrete evidence exists to support any of these hypotheses. One potential location is an anomaly known as Bimini Road, also known as the Bimini Wall. Bimini Road was discovered on September 2, 1968, by J. Manson Valentine while he was diving in three fathoms (5.5 meters) of water off the northwest coast of North Bimini Island, one of the islands that comprises the Bahamas. He encountered an extensive "pavement," which was later found to be made of noticeably rounded stones of varying size and thickness. The stone pavement forms a northeast-southwest linear track. Since Valentine's discovery, the Bimini Road has been visited and examined by geologists, avocational archaeologists, professional archaeologists, anthropologists, marine engineers, innumerable divers, and many other people.

During on-site assessments, investigators have found two additional pavement-like, linear features that lie parallel to and shoreward of the Bimini Road. Interestingly, the discovery of the walls or roads off Bimini Island coincided with the time frame in which Edgar Cayce, the Sleeping Prophet, predicted that Atlantis would be rediscovered. Cayce said that Atlantis had a civilization that was technologically superior to our own, and that its last surviving islands had disappeared in the area of the

Caribbean some ten thousand years ago. Cayce insisted that the sunken continent would be rediscovered in 1968 or 1969, and that a portion of an Atlantean temple would be found underwater in the Bahamas. Cayce also said that an ancient healing spring would be rediscovered on Bimini Island. The discovery of the Bimini Road has been touted by believers of Cayce's prophesies as proof that Cayce was right.

Another astounding archeological find that may be related to Atlantean technology was a device discovered somewhere between the island of Crete and Greece by sponge divers in 1901. It is known as the Antikythera mechanism and may be the world's oldest analog computer. The object, which was first thought to be a navigational device, was found in an ancient shipwreck. It was encased in a wooden box and is over two thousand years old. Since this kind of technology wasn't even thought to be around until about 1575, the complexity of this instrument stymied scientists. When they looked inside of the box using x-rays, they discovered that the box contained a series of interworking bronze gears. The functioning and relationship of the gears has provided great insight into many fields of science. Not only does it show the interrelations of the planets in our solar system as they rotate around the sun, but the device also tracks astrological data relative to planetary movement in and out of the different astrological houses, much like what you would see in an astrology chart.

In the concentric layout of the main city of Atlantis, sectors were utilized for hydroponic gardening. The water came from a desalination process using a form of electrophoresis, which is the electrically induced movement of particles. The electricity was generated from the surrounding water, and the salt extracted was used for food preservation. A unique method of hydroponics enabled the Atlanteans' plants and vegetables to grow to massive sizes, so more people could be fed from less farming space.

Atlantean technology did not end there. They used a crystalline, or subtle, energy, which was provided by a global network of grids made of generator crystals, as well as natural geologic formations. This grid communicated to the Atlanteans the conditions around the planet, as well as geologic and seismic anomalies. By "reading" changes in the electromagnetic

grid, the Atlanteans were able to predict seismic activity, volcanic eruptions, changing weather patterns, and even certain celestial events. The
Maori people in Rotorua, New Zealand, follow this practice even now.

Further, the Atlanteans' crystalline grid dispersed constant energy,
which was harvested and used for other applications. The layout of the
grid was based on angulations of fifteen degrees both above and below
the ground. At the heart of the city's complex, at an exact confluence of
five major ley lines, was a main crystalline generator, which was used to
store the power that was naturally generated from the earth.

The Atlanteans understood the concept of electromagnetic energy and
the idea that light holds information. The technology they derived from
these concepts is similar to our current technology of fiber optics, only the
Atlanteans took it to an entirely new and higher level of understanding.
They kept their records in laser-induced spheres of light that held immeasurable amounts of data, going back through millennia, about the existence
of the Atlantean people. These records could be accessed by the individual
practiced consciousness for purposes of learning and healing.

In their complexes, the Atlanteans had different chambers in
which light was utilized at different individual frequencies, as well as
at combined frequencies. There was a regeneration chamber much like
what the Lemurians had, but which used entirely different frequency
sets, or harmonic combinations. The harmonics in the chambers were
comprised of light, color, and sound. Their healing chambers used
spectrums of light that arced over the body and attuned it to corrected
frequencies in order to reorder the body's particulates. This process
brought immediate healing and corrected harmonic issues that had
been causing the body distress. Another chamber held a large alabaster
table. In this chamber, the energy field of the body could be read and
corrected for specific anomalies. Other chambers contained generators
and a library of information.

The Atlanteans had flying machines that were similar to modern
machines. These machines were much like the Vimana referred to in
ancient Indian texts. The craft were propelled by reverse magnetic technology, in which a rotating central core produced energy. This core was
surrounded by a shell that rotated in the opposite direction, or polarity.

A third shell rotated with the same polarity as the core. This arrangement not only generated ongoing energy, but also maintained the balance of the craft, similar to the way a gyroscope does in current rocket ships and other aircraft.

Across the Atlantis city complex was a rail system fueled by electro-magnetic-resistance technology. This technology used a magnet structure that resisted gravity and created propulsion at the same time, hence moving the cars. This technology was self-sustaining, as were most of the Atlantean inventions.

The Atlanteans domesticated large animals, such as elephants. One of the more interesting aspects of their animal training was their work with dolphins. The Atlanteans were able to understand the chattering, tonal language of the dolphins and could communicate with these creatures. The dolphins were used to communicate across the waters to other Atlanteans who were settled in far-away outposts. (Dolphins today still speak the same ancient language of their ancestors, and when they are finally understood, they will be able to fill in huge gaps of our world history.)

Atlantis was not located in a singular locale. While it is true that the major city was very much as it was described by Plato, there were Atlantean settlements virtually across the globe. These settlements reached from the Atlantic Ocean, where the main city was constructed, to the Canary Islands, the African continent, Antarctica (where one day a pyramid will be discovered below the ice), Polynesia, parts of Asia, and southern Mexico.

There were two factions of people in Atlantis: those of a pure intention and great, high conscious awareness, and another smaller, but very powerful group who were hedonistic, egocentric, and interested in aggressive, destructive power. It was the conflict between the two factions that was the ultimate cause for the demise of Atlantis.

The first of the two groups of people of Atlantis resembled Pleidians. They were quite tall, with jet black hair and crystal blue eyes. They seemed flawless in their perfectly beautiful appearance. They moved fluidly and gracefully, almost as if their presence was an integral part of their environment. These people were the intuitive, heart-centered part of the population. They were gentle people who worked toward the success of not only the people of their civilization, but also the earth.

The opposition, the more hedonistic faction of the population, were blond-haired with brown eyes. These people were of only moderate height, but they were very physically strong. They were aggressive and self-serving by nature and in many ways not as consciously evolved as the black-haired Atlantean beauties.

Looking at the vast difference in the Atlantean people, one might consider that two very different root races joined together at some point to form a vast society, but that their inherent genetic conflicts and differences were the society's ultimate downfall. The conflicts between the two groups are an excellent example for our world today, where differing political and religious views create constant conflict in certain parts of the world. We would be well served to learn from the Atlanteans' example and not allow conflicts to destroy the earth and us, its inhabitants.

As struggles of ego and power overtook peaceful Atlantis, the society was further divided into factions of extreme beliefs. Those who wanted to control the society began to organize into deadly squads of destruction. These groups intended to wipe out those of a more peaceful nature, as their goals had become the promotion of individual importance and recognition, rather than doing what was needed to benefit the society.

During the escalation of differences, there was an individual called Lian, who was of the blonde, brown-eyed group of Atlanteans. Lian led a rebellion in order to gain power over the vast resources of the Atlantean civilization. He and four accomplices raided the main crystalline-generator facility and attacked the workers there in a brutal effort to take control of the entire power grid. In the process of the scuffle, the main generator crystal was knocked out of alignment with the grid. As the angle of the main generator changed, a huge release of energy occurred, causing a chain reaction across the electromagnetic earth grid. Since the grid was built along the ley, or energy, lines of the earth, the release of energy traveled across the grid, amplifying the energies and causing a chain of seismic reactions. These reactions evoked massive earthquake activity that literally shook Atlantis into the ocean.

Some of the outlying settlements survived. With no home to return to, the survivors migrated to safer lands. One of those places was ancient Egypt, where the refugees brought information about their technologies, sharing that information with those in leadership in exchange for equality in their new location. The Atlanteans also migrated to other areas of the planet, including Teotihuacan in Mexico, the coast of southern Mexico, the inland of the United States, the Polynesian Islands, and the coasts of Japan and Antarctica. The Canary Island settlement remained partially intact for some time and was inhabited for several hundred years.

The destruction of Atlantis first happened around seventeen thousand years ago. There were two more events that ultimately finalized the destruction of their empire, which never really recovered after the first most powerful series of events.

Evidence of Atlantean technologies can be found in petroglyphs and pictographs on rocks around the world. It can also be found in some of the hieroglyphs and stone panels left by ancient Egyptians. Further evidence is the locations of sacred sites across the globe; these sites are positioned at exact, predictable intervals measurable by longitude and latitude. Similarities abound in their interior and exterior features, the mathematics and geometry of their construction, the stonecutting techniques in evidence, and the layouts of the sites, including the angles of their pyramids. These various sacred sites also exhibit the astronomical alignments based upon planetary placement in the sky at certain times, as well as alignments to solstices, equinoxes, and other important events in astronomy.

• • •

The information in this chapter describes only some of the available evidence supporting the existence of ancient civilizations that were consciously aware of dimensions beyond the third dimension and of the literal creative processes of reality. The evidence, both factual and mythical, of periods of high consciousness is overwhelming. No one with any intelligence can deny the possibility that there is much, much more to these ancient puzzles. Even the suggestion that there is more that we don't know substantiates the possibilities of civilizations and awareness far beyond anything we can imagine in our current state of consciousness.

The next chapters explain how the ancients accessed higher knowledge and were able to apply that knowledge to their earthly experiences. They explain how we can walk through the doors to the infinite that lies beyond our limited, third-dimension perceptions of reality. You will also learn how we can use this timeless information in the current now to create a greater reality and experience within our inner and external worlds. Further, you will begin to understand why the need for expanded consciousness is part of our survival mechanism—how, as conscious beings, we achieve higher awareness when we must survive devastation created by our own hands in periods of darkness. It is time to enter the light again, and we have already begun to do so.

Meditation 2

Infinite Awareness

All of creation is within you and around you. Look deeply into this visual representation, for it is a multilayered depiction of all creation. Somewhere deep within that vast reality, you exist as an integral part, holding a unique place. Without you, it does not exist, nor do you exist without it.

You, your imaginings, and your perceptions are the root of your reality. Know that you can draw upon the infinite to create anything that you need or desire. Awareness of this truth is the key to unfolding your infinite consciousness. As you experience these symbols, let your body feel this possibility until you no longer feel resistance anywhere within.

Chapter Three

Beyond the Quantum

The Evolution of Consciousness

*I am the light that is over all things. I am all: from me all came forth,
and to me all attained. Split a piece of wood; I am there. Lift up the
stone, and you will find me there.*
— FROM THE GOSPEL OF THOMAS

The statement above is said to be the words of Jesus. What did he
mean? How is it possible that anything can be everywhere?

What did the ancients know that we have forgotten? How can we not
only see beyond the third dimension and into our infinite being, but also
interact with all of creation? Not only did the ancients know the basic
construct of all reality, but they also left us keys to remembering the construct. Those keys are the worldwide tapestry of what we now call sacred
sites. What the ancients left shows us everything about creation and our
relationship within it. But how does our relationship work?

The best way to explore these concepts is to begin at the beginning,
with the genesis of our world and all reality as we know it. What we
must understand is that there wasn't only one beginning. The process of
creation is ongoing. In every tiniest bit of time, every bit of reality is constantly recreating itself. We are being reinvented constantly. There have
been countless beginnings, advents of creation, and geneses of worlds.
And all of these events are directly related to consciousness.

Consciousness heightens as the internal process of creation expands and greater light exists. Creation remembers everything, always. Once we become familiar with this internal process of creation, we can begin to explore the possibilities that are inherent within us.

Our earth has had numerous beginnings. Humanity as we know it is relatively new in the scheme of creation, and yet something inside of us calls to the infinite, like an inner navigation system preset to find the way home. How many of us have had the feeling that we needed to return home, but can't quite remember where home is? We can't remember because home is constantly recreating itself, and we are part of that ongoing creation process.

Humanity has been through changes of all kinds, survived cataclysmic events, and evolved in its skills and technologies, its awareness of possibilities, and even in less tangible ways as something inside of us calls to be remembered. What is it that we are trying to remember, and how do we find it?

Finding the answers to these questions is simple. The best way to get to a clear understanding, though, is to go to the heart of creation.

When the Masters and I worked together and I became more familiar with the cosmic processes, it seemed like they were teaching me in a nonlogical way. I felt like they were teaching me little parts of a bigger puzzle, and I didn't quite get how all the pieces fit together. I never asked them about that. If I didn't understand, I just requested that they show me or teach me what to do. I had a lot of questions, but the truth is, I was so awed, so grateful for what was happening, I didn't want to interrupt the natural occurrence of their presence with a lot of stupid human questions, so to speak. I mean, really, here were holographic beings in my living room, teaching me about light, creation, consciousness, healing, and more. It was awe-inspiring. But I still had questions.

When we learn about metaphysics, those things outside of measurable science, we are told that we are light. We are told that we have to be the moment. We are told that there is no time, there is no space, and that we are part of everything and everything is within us. When I was told these things, I thought it sounded like a lot of tired rhetoric, and yet, deep inside of me, I knew there was truth in those words. So I asked the

Masters, over time, to show me what all of these things were about. And they did—by taking me to the very beginning of creation.

When this happened, my reality shifted instantly, and I was immersed in a tumultuous array of darkness and light. The power of this behemoth of nothingness was wondrous. I could hear the crackling of static sparking and arcing as energy was used and re-created. I could feel the static all through my body, so much that I thought I would fly apart. But only my consciousness was there. I couldn't possibly come apart because I wasn't in my body at all. I could see and feel this great mechanism of creation literally pulsing and moving. It expanded and contracted, and as it did, it moved very slowly in the nothingness. I felt as if I were in the belly of a huge monstrous creature.

The Masters teach by immersion. They don't tell you anything. They take you to the middle of your own questions and immerse you there. You are literally in the midst of both the questions and the answers. The experience becomes part of you—not in the normal way of learning, but really, truly part of you. You receive instant knowledge of every aspect of the answer to your question. The knowing is so complete that there are no words for it. It is a full sensory experience, something even more than visceral.

I remember, early on, trying to find language for what the Masters were teaching me. I had no scientific background or even a frame of reference for what I was experiencing. When I tried to explain to my friends what was going on, they looked at me like I had two heads. One day, a friend of mine said, "Meg, I didn't understand what you said any more the tenth time you said it than I did the first time!" Lacking words, terminology, I was repeating myself over and over in a vain effort to share my experiences.

Essentially, I had to learn an entirely new way of communicating. Where possible, I researched information relative to my lessons. What I found was astonishing. What I was learning was actually—at least partially—known to science in the form of string theory, the M theory, quantum physics, particle physics, theoretical physics, and more. So, like Merlin, I began living backwards, looking for ways to communicate what I knew. And every single day the Masters showed me more. They are still showing me more. So in the best language I can offer for something that is without boundaries or definable by a single thought or word, I want to share at least the basics of what I have learned. This information is as I experienced it. I haven't added anything to it except references to existing scientific theory or reference materials. If you would like to learn more of the science end of it, please see the bibliography at the back of this book.

A Different Kind of Genesis

Reality as we know it didn't always look like it does now. In the beginning of creation, dense matter didn't exist. Reality was a massive, nebulous mass of energy. That energy was very dark and empty, and yet, somehow, it was alive. The mass moved with a predictable rhythm. It writhed. It pulsed. Within it was sound, light, and a constantly changing array of colors, as the light flashed in and out of existence. The mass had awareness that wasn't in the form of words and thoughts. Its awareness was more of an internal, reactionary responsiveness to its own existence.

As the original mass experienced events within itself, it responded to those experiences. These reactions were the very beginning of consciousness.

Each time the mass writhed, energy was used. As the energy was expended, there was a frictional response, which resulted in the creation of more energy. The friction worked like static electricity. When you scoot your feet on the carpet and then touch the doorknob, a spark occurs, and a tiny shock stings your hand. In the same way, the energy created by the friction within the mass manifested as sparks of light. To give you another illustration, think of the electricity created when frictional reactions of one kind or another are generated from the power of water, heat, or even nuclear materials. When those reactions take place, energy—or power, as we call it—is the result.

Whatever the source, energy pulses in regular frequencies, just as creation does. Power that we generate is harnessed and sent to us in a variety of ways. When electricity escapes from its source, such as from wires or generators, it sparks or arcs. Both the sparks and arcing are visible as flashes of light of varying color and intensities. If we happen to be touching the source as the power escapes, we can feel the pulse of that energy in the form of an electrical shock. The energy system of creation is much like this shock, but creation's energy is, for the most part, electromagnetic. This kind of energy is of a higher frequency, or faster pulse, than the electricity we know, but the principles of its creation and expression are similar to those of electricity. We can feel electromagnetic energy in our bodies, and it can be used and directed for a multitude of purposes.

As this cycle occurred over and over within the mass, nearly all of the space in the heart of the mass became filled with light. As the light was created and expended, it popped with electromagnetic energy. As the light grew in volume, it pushed the original dark mass farther and farther away from its center.

Thus, the mass that we call creation began to expand outward from its center as its internal activity grew and changed all the time. And as the original mass was pushed farther and farther outward from its center of origin, the center became thinner and thinner. The mass began to take shape of a toroid, which looks much like a huge doughnut, except that the center wasn't empty—yet.

There came a point in its expansion when the mass of light energy outsized the original mass of darkness, and there was less and less room for balance between the two. The internal pressure became intense. As the intensity escalated, not only did the newly created light push the original mass outward, but it also illuminated the darkness. Ultimately, the internal pressure of the expanded light energy reached a point of critical mass, and a shift of cosmic proportions occurred. The hole in the center opened completely, and because the hole was denser and heavier than the dark, original mass of creation, the mass collapsed upon the newer, lighter form of reality, over the top and down through the newly opened hole in the center. In short, the light became greater in volume and intensity than all of the darkness combined.

In the instant that the darkness fell upon the light, the light was pulverized, fragmented into incalculable numbers of splinters and flung outwardly in a spiral motion. The fragmented light was dispersed in every direction. As the light traveled, the darkness became more illuminated. Now it was lit from the outside as well as from its interior.

A natural spiral in outer space (photo courtesy of NASA.gov)

From the moment of collapse came an expansion of reality. *Individual consciousness* was born in the form of particles of light.

While the light sped outward, it reacted to its experiences. Its frequencies changed, which in turn changed its color and sound frequencies. The memories of each and every experience that the particles of the light had had throughout their journey were imprinted into the light. The imprints remained as literal awareness of everything that the light had gleaned from its very first spark of life to each current moment. In other words, as it moved upon its spiral path, the light chronicled virtually everything that it experienced.

Since each particle of light was experiencing an individual journey, each retained a series of unique memories. All of those memories were stored as energy within the light particles and arrayed as a group of frequencies that, combined, *was* the memory. The memory wasn't in literal form in the way that we define memories now. Instead, the memories were stored as pure energy, full packets of information in energetic form. Each particle of information was an energetic set of frequencies that was encoded with light, color, and sound. Energy is light. Light is energy. Within that energy is light in the form of color and sound. When the frequencies are lower, the color is darker, more intense, and the sound has a deep tone. When the frequencies are higher, the color is lighter, softer, and the sound is higher.

The four-sided pyramid is a perfect example of the complete frequency spectrum. The base of the pyramid represents the lower color and sound frequencies, and the apex represents the highest of the high. The frequencies at the very tip of the pyramid are white, which is the same frequency as the source light. In the color spectrum, white contains all color. Those frequencies that are represented at the base of the pyramid are similar to the tones found in the density of solid matter.

This vast collection of information that the particles of light gathered was literally the beginning of the evolution of both individual and mass consciousness.

As the constantly occurring memories became stored within the light, each tiny particle of that light developed as an individual. In other words, based upon its memories and the information it had recorded, each particle of light became a unique set of harmonic frequencies, an individual aspect of the overall consciousness and creation.

Because each fragment of light had had vaguely diverse experiences in its travel, each existed with a memory of reality that was slightly different than any other. Each distinctive set of frequencies and tones became the identifying factor of each fragment of light. Within that uniqueness, individual consciousness was born.

As the fragments of light began to slow from their initial propulsion, the process of natural ordering began. According to *www.Audioenglish.net*, the definition of natural ordering is "the physical universe considered as an orderly system subject to natural (not human or supernatural) laws." Natural ordering is a law of physics that requires that all things find their natural order, like marbles do when they're put in a jar. The marbles will order themselves into the most expedient positions to form the stack. Like marbles in a jar, every fragment of light was attracted toward other particles of similar experience and frequencies.

Natural ordering must also take the path of least resistance. So the particles of light were naturally required to arrange themselves using the least difficult process. And the easiest way to order themselves was for the particles to align according to shape and harmonic frequency. As they came together, the particles and fragments reflected the light around

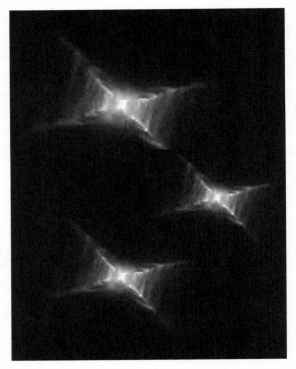

A naturally occurring pyramid form in outer space (photo courtesy of NASA.gov)

them. Ultimately, the arrangements of light ordered together as holograms in the form of four-sided pyramids.

A hologram is a field of light that reflects a scene or an object in a way that appears three dimensional, while maintaining both the amplitude and phase of the light in that field. The scene has no solidity, but is recognizable in every detail.

Every holographic pyramid contained the individual sets of frequencies and memories of all of its combined particles. Thus, each pyramid became an individual consciousness unique from all others.

Consciousness was now taking form.

Each single pyramid contained the memories of its source and the collective experiences of each of the particles within it. As a result, *each pyramid maintained an individual reality, a living consciousness. Each pyramid was aware!*

And they were the first step in the creation of solid mass.

Inside of each pyramid, the energy moved in a spiral motion. As the energy within each pyramid moved up the spiral, it experienced a full spectrum of color and frequencies of energy. In other words, it experienced a complete set of universal energy—full instruction and information about the very moment of its creation and beyond.

The frequencies of the spiral within each pyramid were aligned from the base of the pyramid to the apex, or point at the top. The widest and heaviest frequency fell to the pyramid's base. From there, as the energy within the spiral moved upward, a full spectrum of color was displayed. On up the spiral the energy went, getting lighter and lighter, until eventually the energy returned to the same frequency as its source. As the spiral rotated to the top of the pyramid, it narrowed. Each level of the spiral gradually narrowed to match the shape of the pyramid, and as it did, so did the frequencies all the way through the color spectrum, until the tip of the spiral became white at the apex. White frequencies contain the entire color spectrum and are the exact same frequencies as the original energy that was created by the movement of the original mass of creation. As a result, each pyramid maintained as an inner key to its existence, the memory of its source. (Ah, maybe the ancients *were* on to something!)

Not only did the energy spirals contain all of the possible colors and frequencies of energy, they were also complete sets of sound frequencies.

Motion within the pyramid (graphic by author)

As the spiral inside of each pyramid rotated, a sphere of white energy formed on the pyramid's interior. The sphere was made of the energy that was created by the movement of the spiral. The upward movement of the spiral in combination with the clockwise movement of the sphere served to maintain perfect balance within the interior of the pyramid.

The sphere became a balancing point within the pyramid, much as the axis of a gyroscope balances that device. The sphere also carries the same frequencies as the original source, making it an internal portal through which the pyramid remains accessible and connected to its source.

The process of natural ordering continued, and the holographic pyramids began to order themselves with other pyramids that were familiar in structure and memory. Eight at a time, each apex pointing to the center and each base facing outward, the pyramids structured themselves into holographic octahedrons. With the combined information of each contributing pyramid, each octahedron carried one unique set of harmonic frequencies, or realities. Each octahedron retained consciousness that began as pure light and then took the forms of the pyramid, spiral, sphere, and finally the octahedron and all of the collective experiences from which that octahedron was produced. In the formation of reality, the octahedrons became the particulates, or building blocks, from which all things are created. They became the fabric of the universe.

In the same way that the fragments of light naturally ordered into holographic pyramids, and the pyramids then ordered into octahedrons, the octahedrons began to seek out other octahedrons that had a similar makeup. As they came together, the octahedrons began to align with each other in harmonic relationships. They aligned by order of their flat areas and by opposition of polarity. In the same way that two magnets of opposite polarity, placed end to end, repel each other and thus create a space between them, the flat side of an octahedron, being positive polarity, would align with the flat side of a neighboring octahedron of opposite polarity. These alignments naturally created empty spaces between the particles. These spaces, or null zones, became the balancing factor among the particulates. They also became communication highways throughout the structure of creation.

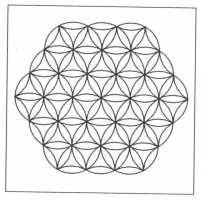

Octahedron arrangement (graphic by author)

The Flower of Life, as depicted on ancient temple walls

The holographic octahedrons ordered next to, above, and below each other. Manifested reality took form as octahedrons aligned by their flat sides, leaving null zones in between. From this arrangement, all reality was formed. As the ordering continued, the variances of frequencies in each set of similar octahedron particles began to order themselves as dimensions of reality. Each dimension formed in the same shape and alignment as the particulates it contained. From the tiniest octahedronal particulates to the dimensional realms, no matter the size or form of creation, all planes of reality were created in this same octahedronal arrangement. Reality had begun to express true form.

Dimensions were produced in every direction and were comprised of the same octahedron shape. Because each contained different sets of harmonics, each dimension had its own set of frequencies—its own reality—based on its position and alignment within the entirety and the internal frequencies of its makeup. The farther outward from its origin of ordering the dimension occurred, the higher its frequencies became. The farther out from its source each dimension was formed, the higher its frequencies were and the more closely it resembled its source light.

The sum of all things looked much like a giant honeycomb. Through time immemorial, the infinite process of creation has often been depicted as this symbol, which was carved by unknown hands millennia ago. Historically, this symbol has appeared in ancient temples, such as the Egyptian Abydos and temple of Osiris, and other initiation temples. And it has also appeared in various buildings, on tapestries, pottery, and other artful creations in Turkey, India, Assyria, Italy, Poland, and other countries. This symbol has been named the Flower of Life by author Drunvalo Melchizedek.

The *unified field theory* describes reality as being of a uniform construction that has both a strong and weak force of energy. Albert Einstein first coined the theory, which basically describes any attempt to unify the most basic particles of creation into a singular speculative framework, or field of energy or matter. Einstein was never, unfortunately, able to prove his theory.

But his theory was right.

While this theory has not, to date, been fully scientifically proven, from what I have been shown by the Masters, it is quite correct in its assumptions. Universally, the strong force of energy is comprised of the particulates. Each holographic octahedron, or particulate, was created of an individual set of harmonic frequencies. Those frequencies were energy. The strength of these combined energies lies in both the uniqueness of their combinations and their collective memory, or consciousness. Their combined consciousness constantly changes because the relationships within reality change from moment to moment and because the light within the particulates automatically keeps a record of the changes.

The weak force of energies, as described in the unified field theory, is comprised of the empty spaces, or null zones, between the octahedrons. The empty spaces serve a twofold purpose. First, the empty zones create balance within the universal structure, and second, the null zones act as hallways for energy to travel. The octahedrons constantly emit electromagnetic energy because they are always experiencing internal change. That energy then moves through the corridors, or null zones, and communicates with all other particulates of creation.

When any individual, group, or series of particulates has an experience, that experience changes the interior makeup of the particulate. The internal frequencies change, and often the polarities of the particulates change too. The internal experience is then communicated externally through the null zones as electromagnetic emissions, which are discharged from the particulates during their interior change. As the electromagnetic communications emitted by the particulates travel along the interior of the null zones, they tell all of the other particulates along the way about the changes that just occurred. The other particulates, receiving the information, respond by reorganizing into different arrangements, or alignments. As this reorganization occurs, with each incident, a new reality is created. In this process, energy is created and expended just like when light was created within the original mass of energy. Ultimately, gravitational waves pulled the ordered particulates closer and closer together, and density occurred. The density, or compaction of the particulate ordering, began to take shape. Reality began to have form and texture. Matter was created and worlds were born in every dimension of reality.

And the process never stops. Further back than we could ever remember, this process of creation has occurred. Creation is continually reinventing itself. Over and over again, the mass of creation has expanded, exploded, and re-created itself. (Currently, we are in an expansive mode.) From the source of all creation, universal evolution had begun, and as it did, the memories of the entire process were collected within the light of every particulate. A constantly growing collective consciousness was born.

From Our Nebulous Source to Dense Reality

The collective particulates continued to order and reorder, and as they did, amazing things began to happen. As the particulates responded by reordering, the harmonic resonance created by the new alignment became new realities. Since not all of the harmonic alliances were the same, different realities formed. The particulates that resided in the outer dimensions, those with higher vibrational frequencies, became unembodied living, universal consciousness. Since it had no definable structure, consciousness remained formless, unfettered by density. The universal consciousness was filled with infinite content and continued to collect the memories of all the particulates as they constantly ordered into new realities. The universal consciousness continues to store and communicate all information, even now.

From the highest level of existence came an inward manifestation of conscious life. The construct of all forms of life was based upon the principles of light. As the creation of reality continued to move inward, back toward the creative center, it did so in spiral form. Due to the weight and compression of each preceding layer, or dimension, of reality, the particulates and the light they contained became denser and denser as the inner dimensions were formed. Therefore, so did the matter.

Because it was created of varying frequencies, each new dimension became a slightly different aspect of consciousness. The higher dimensions carried full awareness of everything in creation, while the more dense dimensions had less and less awareness due to their compression from dimensions above. As density occurred, consciousness became trapped within specific areas of reality.

Beings that are created of the outer realms have little to no density. They are often known as beings of light—infinite creatures living within the consciousness of creation. These beings display their form in arrays of living color. These colors vary, depending upon their dimensional source. As they move it is as if they were created of liquid light. Color flows with every motion of their magnificent reflection of creation. These beings ultimately became a bridge of communication between the lower, denser dimensions and the source, and they are often recognized as our etheric guides.

At different dimensions, or frequency levels, the living consciousness organized as life forms created of different levels of density. Those formed in higher frequencies retained more of the original source information in their awareness. The denser the reality and, therefore, the being, the less source awareness it had. Of course, the information was there, inherent in their being, but due to their density, the information wasn't as readily available to them in the form of awareness. It was at about this point that survival techniques began to develop. Without direct memory of their parts in creation, beings of lower density developed fear and survival skills. Human beings were among the denser creations.

As the manifestation process moved inward, the sixth, seventh, and eighth dimensions—dimensions of great mentality—formed. Those born of these dimensions of the infinite mind became links between the above and the below, between the light and its denser forms. They retain the knowledge of the processes of development of both the outer and inner realms. Their information is stored in symbols created of light, which contain complete expressions of the highest concepts and the tiniest details. These are the symbols described in Chapter One.

No emotionality was retained in the informational realms. The mass of its consciousness and the data it contained became a living reality of stored information known as the conscious mind, or the Akashic Records. There are beings who reside in these intellectual realms. The A Lan Ta group, who spoke through me and taught me and my weekly metaphysical group about the pyramids, were from this area of creation. They were relentless in their teachings and had no patience for anything outside of their mission. Much like *Star Trek*'s Mr. Spock, they did not understand emotionality at all. They could, in fact, be somewhat intimidating.

Further inward in the dimensional construction, below the mental planes, came the emotional planes—those dimensions where existence is based completely upon the expression of emotions. There are levels of the greatest love and of the deepest pain and of every emotion in between. These dimensions comprise the astral plane. It is to the astral plane we often travel in our dreams or when we experience out of body travel.

Even further inward, the third dimension formed. In this dimension began the development of literal physical form. Even though it is constructed from the same source and by the same process as all other levels of creation, due to the density of its makeup, which is caused by the pressure of outer dimensions, life in this realm retains only slight conscious awareness of its origins. That slight awareness is what we sense as need to go home, wherever home is.

Along with life in the third dimension, galaxies formed and within them, checks and balances became a natural occurrence. Everything formed with a spiral motion. Light expresses itself magnificently as nebulae, stars, and other celestial bodies.

The light learned from its original creation experience and began to build structures of balance in order to propagate itself. During these formations, as the original light re-created itself, black holes twisted into existence, draining off excess pressure into parallel realities. Planets, spiraling masses with an abundance of energy at their centers, formed. The surfaces of the forming planets remained mobile around each center, floating upon heated masses of molten debris that had come together to become the dense mass of each planet. In an ongoing effort to balance, vents developed in the surfaces of the lands to continually discharge energy from deep within the planets' centers. On earth, these vents are volcanoes, and energy is discharged in the form of volcanic eruptions. The areas of venting include so-called hot zones such as Yellowstone National Park or Rotorura, New Zealand, where there are hot pools of water, geysers, hot soils, and often the smell of sulphur.

An intensification of gravitational forces developed due to the spiral motion of the forming planets. As everything in creation spiraled toward its center of origin, the pull of gravity increased. With the formation of gravity, another form of balance occurred, and the planets, stars, and other celestial bodies stabilized their patterns of movement and established their orbital positions.

Parallel universes began to take shape, feeding off the excess energies of those universes around them—energies constantly provided through the black holes. Infinite realities spun into existence, each one subsisting on the extra energy of the universes that had formed around it.

Consciousness of different levels continued to be built into each new reality. The consciousness of the realities that developed below the fifth dimension ignorantly began to function outside the consciousness of their source. Those beings borne of these levels logically began to consider themselves as separate aspects of creation. Their density did not allow them to remember their source or anything that had happened since the time of creation. Therefore, without awareness, their access to the collective consciousness became restricted.

Those beings of the third dimension began to create illusions of existence, which grew into a lesser reality than that of the universal, source consciousness. They began to perceive a vast emptiness inside of themselves and were able to grasp only *possibilities* of a greater reality, for they had forgotten their perfection. Even though there remained a tugging memory just in the background of their awareness, they couldn't quite remember what it was they had forgotten.

Beyond the third dimension, even denser realities were formed. The most inner realms were those where the remnants of the primal darkness had fallen. Within these dark realms, the most rank of creatures resided with vileness and hatred, secrets and lies, and feelings of hopelessness. These vile, dark creatures fear everything and take their power from the weak and the dying. They carry the stench of brimstone and worse.

The remnants of the original light did not penetrate beyond the darkness in these deep levels of creation, and the darkness ravaged all remaining hints of light. The darkness struggled to be free of light, manifesting dark warriors: semblances of being that were of a despicable nature. Yet each time the battles raged, the light and those who had manifested of it were victorious. It was during these times that Lucifer fell from the angelic realm, cast out by others. The angelic wars went on for a great time—light fighting dark, perfection fighting evil. And as the wars continued, the light grew in power and strength, and the darkness seethed in its failure to regain its balance against the light.

But the darkness has not prevailed, because each time it rears up, its very motion creates more light. The movement of the darkness caused the same friction that had allowed the light to outgrow the massive darkness in the beginning. The light perpetuated, and from deep within the heart of darkness came yet other inklings of light, reminiscent of their source. A new heart of creation was born, and in this infinite pattern of the creation is the continual promise of cosmic rebirth. By the Mayan calendar, we are coming to another moment of cosmic rebirth in December 2012.

The Difference Between Consciousness and Thought

As human beings, we are aware of our consciousness through our thoughts, but *our thoughts are not our consciousness*. Our thoughts are a series of electrical impulses. They attempt to create logic, to understand and reason through our experiences. Our thinking self is part of our survival mechanism. Our minds plod along, ever diligent, to assure us that we are safe, right, and that everything makes sense—or doesn't.

In our earliest forms of being, we were all telepathic. We retained some awareness of the universal consciousness and had no need for words. We knew instantly what we needed to know—not just with our brains, but also with our entire bodies. Our consciousness brought us a constant stream of information, and we listened. As we evolved, and survival became a forefront concern, our brains began to localize our brain-wave patterning. We started to think about things repeatedly, trying to make sense of what we didn't understand. As our thought patterns became more and more limited by reason, our brains began to use less and less of their full capacity. Because of the new brain-wave patterns, access to our consciousnesses became more and more limited.

Other beings, such as the Lemurians, came into our realities and interbred with us, creating hybrid species that were ultimately integrated into our current biology. Other beings visited our planet from faraway galaxies and also contributed to our gene pool. Based on the Sumerians' writings and the indications that they knew of high technologies, there is much speculation that at least one group of visitors may have come to earth prior to the rise of Sumerian civilization. The blending of those early other-dimensional races and human beings created huge gaps in the archeological timetables, because during those gap times, humanity took large leaps in its evolution. There are gaps of time when "missing links" haven't been found. It isn't likely they ever will be.

As the new humans began to migrate and interbreed, trade, and interact with other humans, some form of communication became necessary. We began to use forms of sound that mimicked the sounds of our environments. Making bird-like sounds, clicking like some insects, grunting and yipping like different animals, and imitating the sounds of nature evolved into recognizable language. These early sounds refined into words. The words were then organized, and speech began. With speech came body language and subtleties. And the mind became more active. The thinking brain was challenged to work differently. It evolved not only because of the need to understand speech, but also because of the need to understand the unspoken, subtle communication behind speech—what speakers really meant. Soon nuances began playing a part in communication as well. How the word was spoken and how the body expressed itself during the speaking of those words had everything to do with what was being said. Multiple forms of communication and more subtle communication levels began to develop.

The mental, thinking self evolved further and further from the conscious self. Information became absolutely defined and grew further away from pure truth. The ego began to weigh in and measure current situations based upon previous experience. When the ego and the logical brain disagreed, the brain began to fill in the gaps with what it already understood, and the illusion of everyday life was born. The ego began to judge, to praise, to confound, and to confuse communication. In the end, we evolved away from our natural telepathic abilities, and the result was a convoluted mess of interpretation-based interaction.

Yet somewhere, outside of our cognitive awareness, deep inside of us, we remembered our origins. We instinctively sought out areas of great energy upon the earth where the energy of the planet flowed in patterns that we now call ley lines. In periods of enlightenment, we began to build on sites where the energies of the ley lines converged. From the bowels of our memory, we drew forth geometries, subtle references to our beginnings. We built pyramids. We created whole cities based upon the mathematics of spirals. All of the angulations and symbols came from the memories of creation inside of us. We created temples and initiation chambers in which we could experience the interrelations of energy harmonically, move out of our perceptions of time and space, and gain insight in aspects of creation.

In those temples and initiation chambers, some of us began to remember at least some of our infinite source. The rites of initiation became a privilege, available only to those of royal descent or those who qualified by meeting certain criteria of advancement, such as priesthood. Others were kept in the dark with no access to, or knowledge of, higher awareness. Interdimensional beings and inter-galactic travelers became our gods, and we gave our power to them because we misunderstood their true identities. Our consciousness evolved, and we created great civilizations, such as Atlantis and Sumeria. We left behind distinct clues for future generations, as well as the keys to understanding those clues. But in darker times of awareness, we forgot what the evidence meant. We left ourselves road maps to lead us back to our origins and to our greater awareness, but we forgot how to read them.

As we further evolved, living upon the earth and doing our best to survive as a species, our infinite awareness took a back seat to our logical brains. It isn't that we completely forgot our origins and greater abilities; instead, the imbalance developed due to the electrical nature of our brains. When we are thinking, our brains work based upon electrical impulses. Neurons fire, and electrical impulses travel along our neuropathways, carrying information to specific parts of our brains. The impulses follow set patterns that we developed during our evolution. Certain parts of our brains evolved to suit particular purposes, such as storing memories, triggering responses, and even controlling our senses. In fact, our brains refined their abilities so well that much of our brain matter seems to serve no purpose at all.

Our consciousness isn't electrical in nature at all. It is *electromagnetic*, much lighter in energy and functioning. Our consciousness isn't limited to our head or our body. It has the ability to travel far beyond our dense bodies, across dimensions and into the infinite. As I found out, our consciousness can cross the barriers of space and time. It moves faster than the speed of light. Our consciousness knows inherently how to access whatever information we need or desire, and it can bring that information to us instantaneously. The problem is that we forgot how to listen. We began to confuse our logical minds with our infinite ones, and soon we couldn't tell the difference between the two. At the same time, our egos and our emotions became a part of the mix. Our emotions contribute hugely to our reactions to every experience. Our emotions are driven by past experiences, physical memories of what we love, what we fear, and everything in between.

Every time we have a mental process, our reaction triggers the release of chemicals throughout our body. The chemicals stimulate our emotions, and our emotions respond by triggering more and different chemical releases. We literally and physically become our perceptions. And this further confuses us!

Our life experiences perpetuate and repeat because there is nothing obvious telling us to change direction or to stop the cycle. We become caught in patterns of behavior and response, and we become unhappy in our experiences.

The most profound results of our evolution away from pure consciousness are twofold. First, we begin to believe that we are separate from all other things. As a result, we are often left feeling afraid and alone in our huge world. We begin to feel helpless, empty, searching for something that we . . . almost . . . remember . . . but can't quite grasp: the memory of our infinite selves.

Second, most of us look externally for answers that will remind us how to fill that emptiness, for instructions to a better way of being, but we never really feel satisfied. That is because the answers we seek are within each of us, not in books, not on the Internet, and not in the opinions or experiences of other people.

How do we reconnect to the awareness that we have lost? Finding the answers to that question isn't as difficult as you might think.

Meditation 3

Co-creation

Imagine the possibility that you are not dependent upon the limited resources of your thinking brain or on any other person or circumstance. You are not separate from all other things. Imagine that you can draw upon the infinite, working in tandem within the One to co-create anything you desire. Allow yourself to become immersed in the creative process, knowing that what is has always been and always will be. There is continuity in everything, and you are part of it.

Chapter Four

We Are the True Trinity

---

*We are infinite beings, unlimited in time and space, but individually
limited by our perception that we are something less.*

The Metascience of Consciousness

As consciousness became condensed into form, the process of creation continued. As our bodies came into being, every particulate
that became the reality of us came together as individual aspects of our
singular consciousness. Every atom, every molecule, every cell contains
the essence of the source. Our source constantly re-creates itself within
us. With the expression of all of the energy that we expend simply by
existing, and further by our thoughts, actions, and words, we communicate to creation our very experiences.

Creation, in turn, responds. The spiral movement of creation continues within us, constantly communicating to us everything that is
happening in creation. At the same time, everything that we are experiencing is communicated to creation. This spiral motion and its infinite
movement are demonstrated mathematically by a formula known as
the Fibonacci sequence and are represented pictorially by the Julia set
on page 88.

In my book, *Pyramids of Light: Awakening to Multi-dimensional Awareness*, I described the Fibonacci sequence as a series of numbers based on
a mathematical sequence beginning with zero; each following number is
the sum of the two preceding numbers. For example:

$0+1=1$, $1+1=2$, $2+1=3$, $3+2=5$, $5+3=8$ . . .

The Julia set (graphic by author)

The numbers in the Fibonacci sequence begin to look like this:
0, 1, 1, 2, 3, 5, 8, 13, 21, 34, 55 . . .

The sequence of numbers continues in a spiraling sequence that goes on infinitely.

In addition, dividing each number in the Fibonacci series by the number that precedes it produces a ratio that stabilizes at about 1.618034, or phi, which is the golden ratio. Nearly all of the sacred sites around the world incorporate the golden ratio.

Often, the Julia sets represent the balance between order and chaos after the Mandelbrot (another mathematical formula) has broken down. The Mandelbrot set pictorially displays images with fractal boundaries that do not simplify at any magnification. In mathematics, as an example, an equation holds firm as long as the sequence of logic remains constant. In fractal geometry, when the breakdown of predictable logical sequences occurs, the result becomes a cascade. The cascade is the uncontrolled, repetitious events that occur when momentum becomes self-reliant and constant within itself. The cascade is the natural form of creation in its spiral motion, often represented by the Julia set.

On July 7, 1996, a crop circle appeared in a wheat field near Stonehenge. The circle was in the form of the Julia set! The crop circle was formed with 151 circles, and it had a length of 385 feet (117.3 m) from north to south. This crop circle was a masterpiece of art and science. Particularly notable was the fact that *all* 151 of the circles that comprised the crop circle rotated clockwise in the wheat. (It is my contention that crop circles are not created by UFOs, but by consciousnesses transcending the dimensional barriers. In other words, consciousnesses being projected from other realities into ours create pictorial representations of science, principles of life, energy, and a whole lot more.)

We have the very same golden spiral in our heads. The spiral is centered at the pineal gland and also incorporates the pituitary gland and the hypothalamus. As the spiral moves outward, it coils across the corpus callosum within the central brain area. When we learn to access the spiral within us, we can instigate higher, more finely vibrating brain frequencies and, thus, open the doors to higher conscious awareness.

We have multiple levels of brain-wave activity, each serving a particular purpose in our functioning. For example, we use delta brain waves when we sleep, alpha brain waves for relaxation, and theta brain waves when we meditate. Sixth-sense activities occur mostly when we have accessed our theta brain waves.

Beyond the theta level, we begin to use gamma waves, very fine brain waves that create a unification of energy across our brains. When we use our

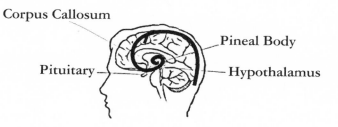

The golden spiral within the human head (graphic by author)

gamma brain-wave functioning, the gamma waves unify the electrical and electromagnetic circuitry within our brains. The gamma waves radiate outward from the center of our brain in a uniform way, uniting parts of the brain that do not work together in our current states of consciousness. In the moment that we achieve unification of our electrical and electromagnetic functioning, an interesting thing happens. The door to the infinite opens, and we immediately leap into higher consciousness. We become aware of realities that are beyond our third-dimension awareness. In the moment we leap into gamma consciousness, we awaken to multidimensional awareness! I call this multidimensional awareness our seventh sense. From there, we are no longer aware of limitations of time, limitations of space, or any other type of limitations.

There are three levels of gamma consciousness. The first level is *initiation*. The initiation level is accessed at the end of the widest point of the spiral, located at the back of the head, between the occipital bones. When we enter the initiation phase of gamma-wave activity, we step just inside the door of higher consciousness and experience initial awareness of other realities. We may see or experience glimpses of other realities, colors, geometric shapes, or other forms of living energy. We might have impressions of other beings or realities that come and go in a flash out of the corners of our eyes, but which we can't quite focus on to make the impression a reality. In other words, the momentary flash is more of a suggestion than a definite image or experience.

The second level of gamma-wave functioning occurs at the crest of the spiral, the widest part of the exterior curve, right at the crown of the head. This level is called *communion*. With practice, during the communion phase of gamma consciousness, we may actually interact within other-dimensional realms while experiencing a full range of senses. It is at the communion level that our seventh sense opens. From this level of functioning, we can reach beyond the barriers of time and space, literally visiting places in the past or future, other dimensions, and even faraway galaxies. It is this level of awareness that Enoch, Moses, Jesus, the Buddha, and other historic Masters remained connected to, gathering wisdom and even using the infinite information and energies to create miracles.

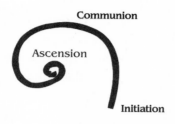

The three levels of gamma consciousness (graphic by author)

The communion aspect of gamma consciousness is the reason many religions require the head to be covered. We are told that covering our head is a sign of respect, but the truth is that covering our crown somewhat restricts the energy flow there. When the energies are restricted, the energy of our crown is not as open, and therefore, we remain ignorant to the more subtle information that is available to us.

I have spent innumerable time in the communion phase of gamma consciousness. There, I have met beings who have taught me about worlds of creation and reality that have opened possibilities of life to me that are beyond words. Beings of great light and beauty have come time and again to teach me about creation, consciousness, healing, and even how to learn not with my brain, but with the particles of light that are within each of us.

In the beginning, it seemed that I was being taught in fragments that didn't make sense. The Masters showed me forms of light and taught me how to manipulate them into different shapes and colors. They showed me how energy can be used and changed in order to literally change one form of matter to another. They showed me how everything is interconnected and that all creation is infinitely choreographed to a constantly changing reality. They instructed me in the recognition of energy patterns and frequencies in the human body, showing me how discordant harmonics literally lead to illness. Further, they showed me how to reharmonize the energies to create wellness.

They taught me so much, so fast, that my sense of reality was challenged. The Masters told me that all chaos is nothing more than a perceived entanglement of simplicities. I began to realize the extent of the illusions that we create in third-dimension living, as the logical mind and the ego battle and work together to convince us that everything is just fine, when it is not. My entire value system changed. The little things were no longer important. In fact, neither were the things that I'd thought were huge or vital to my experience. I learned just how simple everything is.

For the longest time, I had no idea what I was learning. Pieces and flashes of complete realities came and went. Profound awareness of many subjects and technologies flowed through me. I had no idea what much of it meant, but I kept taking myself into the awareness. Each time I did, the Masters were patiently waiting for me to return. I didn't allow myself to become frustrated in the need to know. I never, ever asked how, why, what—anything other than "Show me."

And then one day I got it. I can't say understood, because none of my experience with the Masters would make sense as long as I tried to understand what was happening. Instead, the knowledge became part of my very being. It has no limits and cannot be defined as singular concepts, because everything is related—all of it, infinitely.

Access to this state of awareness is something that happens out of humility. The awareness that comes of it is beyond any single human being. That awareness is timeless and unlimited in scope. It is not the stuff of logic, but the entirety of memory that has been held within the light for eons—in fact, forever.

If we have any expectations about how the experience of gamma consciousness will be, the expectations will limit the experience so profoundly that access to gamma consciousness will be impossible. No amount of logical functioning can be used during gamma consciousness.

When we can let go of the sense that we are individuals who are apart from all other things and instead intentionally participate from within the One, our brains are out of the way, our hearts connect, and the experience is euphoric. We are inherently filled with the memory of infinite times and endless reality, and at the same time, we realize that it is all perfect, interwoven, related, and without a doubt, the truth of divinity.

Perceiving from this new state of awareness allowed me to "tap into" the universal memory. I became able to discuss subjects I had never even considered, and was thus able to speak to scientists, physicians, and others about new aspects of their specialties when I had no training in these subjects at all. While I usually haven't had a frame of reference or the terminology for what I've seen or learned, somehow I have been able to find enough words to communicate the information. Rising intelligence seems to be a very desirable side effect of heightened conscious awareness. That being said, we can begin to see how civilizations from the past brought high technologies into a seemingly primitive world. Like me, they simply "tapped into" the universal memory. Or they brought knowledge from the universal memory with them from whatever dimension they came from.

The key here is to understand that technology isn't the ultimate power. Technology is nothing more than a side effect of rising consciousness. Technology may *seem* to give temporary power, but as we know from ancient Egypt, the Sumerians, the stories of Lemuria and Atlantis, and even from current happenings, technology and egos simply don't mix. The combination is destructive and ultimately the demise of every powerful civilization that has ever been.

It seems that the possibilities inherent in using gamma consciousness are limitless as long as we don't try to understand it. The knowledge from gamma consciousness comes as whole knowing. The problem sometimes is finding the vocabulary to express what we see or all of a sudden know because we have reached into other worlds beyond this one, finding far-reaching kinds of awareness and infinite knowledge. This kind of awareness is simply outside of our "normal" frames of reference. Like the shaman and the natives on the shore, in order for us to take even the first step toward unlimited consciousness, we must be willing to accept the possibility that is even exists.

Once we have experienced awareness beyond our human world, there is no going back to ignorant perceptions. Life beyond humanity is vast and limitless. Having experienced this life firsthand, we begin to recognize the illusions in our world. We can recognize subtle energies, people's true motivations, how things are not what they seem, and even how we had convinced ourselves of truths that don't exist. Life becomes a lot "cleaner" without all of the illusions. We begin to see things as they truly are, and doing so brings us freedom, first from our self-imposed illusions and then from those of everyone else. We learn to become conscious observers instead of players in everyone's games. We learn that the drama and trauma of interrelationships is just that. And we can relax, knowing that what is really happening isn't always ours to carry.

Imagine the possibility of being consciously aware of all dimensions of reality at the same time, like an infinitely harmonized musical chord that is resonant across all levels of creation. Imagine that while having that awareness, it becomes integrated into the human experience. The human and the divine intertwine as the universal question of infinite possibilities. This is the true mergence of divinity and humanity. In this convergence of humanity and infinite consciousness, we realize that we are the god that we seek and that anything we have ever sought has also sought us.

The possibilities are endless, because information is transferred not in a linear format, but holographically. Full sets of information—sets that are both a whole concept and every imaginable detail of that concept—come in a flash of whole-body understanding. The brain in its electrical state can't conceive of this type of information, but from a state of gamma consciousness, we have the ability to realize that anything is possible and everything is available to us.

The third level of gamma brain-wave activity is the *ascension point.* It is located at the smallest point of the spiral around the pineal gland. Medically speaking, allopathic doctors and scientists don't seem to know much about the purpose of this gland. But it is at this tiny place in the center of our heads that we connect to infinite reality, back to our source consciousness in which we are everything and everything is us.

At this point of consciousness, we lose awareness of any aspect of separateness, and our experience is the perception of pure, golden light. We become aware of everything in existence as if we *are* the infinite consciousness. In that state, it is true, we *are* the infinte, yet our sense of individual awareness still remains. In the ascension consciousness, our sense of individuality is very different. Individual consciousness takes on the form of simple awareness, nothing more. No linear mentality, no justification or judgment, no ego—just observations of infinite awareness. It is like floating in pure bliss. We no longer have any sense whatsoever of our physical form. What we see, hear, feel, know is pure light. The third gamma state is a level of awareness that generally only those touted as Masters throughout history have achieved, but it is possible for anyone to experience.

I've experienced the third gamma state on several occasions. What I realized in those moments was that there was a choice: rejoin the infinite or remain as a mere mortal. There was no middle ground. I have to say that deciding to return to simple humanness after being in the ascension consciousness is very, very difficult. Ascension consciousness is a state of pure, unadulterated love and absolute bliss, yet when I was there, some part of me realized two things.

The first was that this was how ascension is accomplished. Many of us spend a lifetime thinking that we need to ascend to some higher realm by a process of deeds and lessons, positive action, healing ourselves, or achieving specific goals. But to ascend is really just to return in consciousness back to our source.

The second thing I realized was that being human is not really anything but a spiritual vacation. I realized that being human affords us experiences that we don't have in light form: to be touched, to feel the depths of emotion, to have the opportunity to experience life from specific instances, each with a purpose and each with infinite possibilities. As human beings, we can experience touch, sounds, sight, and the love of one person for another. We can experience what is tangible. There is great pleasure in the human experience and also great pain. It is the balance between the pleasure and the pain that we seek, and in that learning process is our humanity. In this way, we are like fledgling universes emitting light in our beginnings. We can relax into our natural evolution as beings of light, or we can resist, allowing our darkness to overwhelm us into submission and stagnancy. The infinite being is who we really are. Knowing that the human life is only temporary, and there is truly nothing to fear about leaving it at some point, is extremely freeing.

Pictorially, our mergence with the universal consciousness when we are in the gamma states of consciousness looks like two pyramids—one upright, one inverted—combined to form a star tetrahedron. The upright pyramid represents our individual consciousness; the inverted pyramid represents universal consciousness. When combined, the two form a star

The star tetrahedron, comprised of two pyramids, represents the true trinity. The upright pyramid represents our individual consciousness; the inverted pyramid represents universal consciousness. When combined, the pyramids create a third form, a star tetrahedron, which represents the trinity of us, creation, and the combination of us and creation. (Graphic by author)

tetrahedron, representing a true trinity: us, creation, and the combination of us and creation. Or, as some might say, the Father (creation), the Son (us) and the Holy Spirit (the combination of creation and us).

The first, upright pyramid is us: individual forms of consciousness brought into pure geometric form. This form is truth, as consciousness developed in its evolution. We can literally project our awareness into the form of the upright pyramid to experience ourselves as pure consciousness without the distractions of our external world. When we enter the pyramid, our breath becomes cold, and we begin to hear a tone. That tone is our individual frequency. There is no other being or thing in all of creation with the same tone.

Remember in Chapter Three when we talked about how the light came together into the pyramid form, creating individual sets of consciousness? Well, when we enter a pyramid by projecting our awareness inside, we are simply, for the moment, returning our consciousness to its most basic form. Once inside the pyramid, we also feel a great sense of calm. This exercise is an excellent way to safely practice having an out-of-body experience, because moving our awareness inside the pyramid structure means we are literally entering the form of creation. We can't get lost.

The inverted pyramid signifies the universal consciousness, or creation. Like a satellite dish, it is collecting information about everything, all of the time, on every level of creation. Projecting our awareness into the inverted pyramid, we find that the energy feels very busy, even chaotic. There seems to be a lot of movement in the energy, and it is difficult to "focus" on what our impressions are. That is because the universal consciousness is constantly changing.

When the inverted pyramid is combined with the upright pyramid form, an amazing series of events happens. The spheres inside of each pyramid merge, and as they do, they first flatten and then, all of a sudden, form a singular sphere that joins the two forms energetically. The two pyramids harmonize together. In this way, a true trinity is formed. We become the upright pyramid, creation, and the combination of us and creation—all at once.

This combination represents how we are God, and God is us. Whatever you want to call the Creator, on this level, it is all the same. In this form of consciousness, we literally and intentionally join creation with our awareness. When we do this, we free ourselves of everyday and self-created distractions and enter pure consciousness. From here, we can travel anywhere in time and space, because as we leave our limited perceptions of the logical mind and the third dimension, we find that there is no time and there is no space. We just are, just like we have always been.

When the ancients buried their dead inside of pyramids, they were, consciously or subconsciously, placing the deceased into the most basic form of geometric truth. They were literally returning the person to the basic format of creation, so that the soul could be re-created, reborn in the afterlife. The ancients believed pyramids to be portals to the other worlds. How right they were! On some level of awareness, our ancient predecessors knew what they were doing when they built tombs and sacred sites in the form of the four-sided pyramid and the Golden Mean. They were reminding us just who we are and of what we are capable. All over the planet, they left us sets of instructions about our very essence. They left us examples of the very fundamental nature of creation and of who we are in the infinite relation to it. Sadly, we have become so caught up in the understanding of the logistics of these sites that we have completely missed the obvious: when we visit these sites, we are looking at the very basis of creation in the mirror.

Consciousness and DNA

We have already learned that universal consciousness is present in every particle of our being, but how does our state of consciousness affect our physical being? Is there a connection? If so, how does it work, and how can we use that connection to our benefit?

In each cell of our physical being, DNA is present. DNA is our complete instruction manual. It dictates how we look, our personal characteristics, our personalities, and often even how we react to stimuli in our lives. DNA carries the information of our entire lineage as well.

DNA looks much like a twisted ladder. As with the spiral, which occurs all throughout nature, we can often find natural illustrations of DNA in our more mysterious worlds such as the magnificent DNA nebula, found near a massive black hole in the center of the Milky Way galaxy. DNA is a tiny part of who we are physically, but the encoding that it carries is infinite in its scope.

The DNA nebula is about eighty light years long. It's about 300 light years from the super massive black hole at the center of the Milky Way. The nebula is nearly perpendicular to the black hole, moving out of the galaxy at a quick clip—about 620 miles per second. (Photo courtesy of NASA/JPL-Caltech/ M. Morris [UCLA])

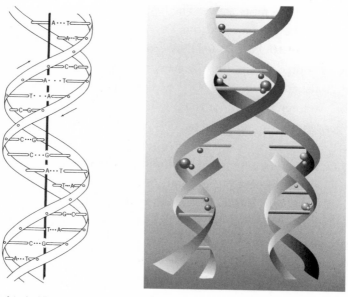

A typical DNA strand   DNA replicating (photo © anto titus/iStockphoto)

Our DNA is comprised of four amino acids: adenine (A), thymine (T), guanine (G), and cytosine (C). The different combinations of these amino acids determine the instructions the DNA gives to us.

Remember how energy re-creates itself? How it begins at the source, changing frequencies and using itself up, and, by its consumption, creates more energy? DNA is like that. DNA constantly replicates itself in a process reminiscent of the process of creation. The two halves of the DNA spiral split into two, and new strands are formed. Each time the DNA reproduces, it splits and duplicates itself exactly to form two new molecules. Each strand of the original molecule can then act as a template for the synthesis of a new, complementary DNA molecule.

In another mirroring of creation, DNA strands have their own unique energy fields. Each tiny DNA strand emits a field of electromagnetic energy, like a soft glow that surrounds the strand.

When we access gamma consciousness, the glow around our DNA expands, and the electromagnetic field around the DNA becomes larger, wider, and even more active. The higher we go in gamma consciousness, the larger the glow around our DNA strands becomes. At the point of ascension, the fields of our DNA expand so far that they unify into one field of source energy, uniting every particle of our bodies with the vast consciousness of creation. It is at that point that everything becomes light; we lose our sense of the physical, and our physical bodies are no longer separate in our awareness.

At the same time our DNA responds to our greater awareness with greater emissions activity and communication within our DNA strands also changes. In previous generations, communication along the DNA strand was quite linear. Messages, in the form of electrical impulses, traveled up one leg of the DNA ladder or the other and went from one segment of the chain to the next in straight-line communication. As a natural course of our fast-forward evolution as human beings, a few years ago, the communications within our DNA began to arc, skipping over one or more segments and even turning on some segments that were previously "asleep." Currently, communication in some people's DNA is not only arcing up single sides of the ladder, but is also arcing from one side to the other. As this happens, the electromagnetic emissions coming from our DNA respond by expanding, changing intensity, and even contracting at times.

DNA and consciousness are directly related. What one does, the other follows. The result of this phenomenon is that consciousness begins to expand as DNA expands. This is why so many people seem to be spontaneously "awakening." What is truly occurring is the spontaneous raising of consciousness as part of human evolution, not so much on the physical level as on the levels of conscious awareness.

The more we use our higher awareness, the more our DNA awakens and vice versa. As more and more of us use our high knowing, more and more people will also be able to use theirs. Because we humans are all interconnected by virtue of our particulates, we are constantly sending and receiving signals about our experiences throughout creation. Creation, in turn, tells every particle of itself what is happening, and a new reality is formed. In other words, we are hardwired into creation, our divine source. Because of this connection, our physical being has inherent instructions to return to its divine state. Because of our inherent mutual interconnectedness with creation and, thus, each other, using our higher awareness actually changes our reality. Each time we use it, the light within us responds. In turn our DNA reacts to the changes, giving further instructions for us to continue to evolve. And those changes in reality enable even more of us to use higher awareness. And the spiraling action of creation and re-creation continues.

Meditation 4

As Above, So Below — Creation Is Within Us

Consider that all forms of creation exist both outside and inside you. What does this possibility mean to you as the creator of your own reality? How can you affect everything within and around you for positive change? Listen for how the infinite speaks within you—beyond your thoughts, beyond your perceptions. Listen deeply. Find the rhythm within you, and let your awareness ride it.

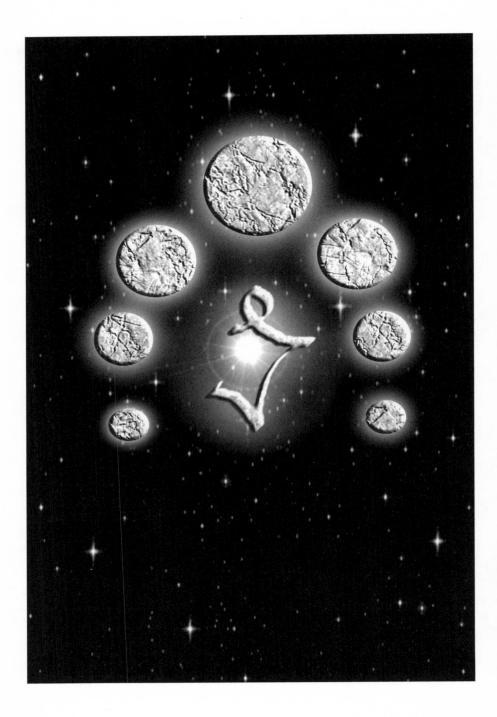

Chapter Five

Becoming the Change

Creating the Reality We Want

Without practical application, everything in the preceding pages would be just a lot of interesting information. But what if we could apply this higher knowing to everyday life? What if we could use our consciousness within the construct of creation to create the kind of reality that we desire? We can!

Each time we make a choice in our life, we change our awareness, the literal path of our consciousness. Our consciousness changes frequencies in response to our choices as it travels through the areas between the particulates, the very construct of creation. As it does, the energy of our choice communicates to creation, which then brings to our life experience the results of our choice. In the moment our choice is made, and our consciousness communicates that choice into the construct of creation, we actually change all that we are and all of reality simultaneously.

Just like what happened in the beginning of creation, as light re-created itself over and over again, the energy of our intention re-creates itself over and over again as it travels, all the while getting stronger and stronger, until ultimately, a solid reality is formed. As the messages are received by the particulates, the particulates begin to rearrange in response, creating a different set of harmonic relationships. These new relationships literally become our new reality.

When we believe that we are stuck and can't change our experiences, our beliefs and the accompanying emotions cause our energy fields to become dense and compressed, holding back the very communications that could have changed our experience, if we had let them. When our energy condenses, it ultimately traps the information of our desires close to us and restricts the information from getting the message out to creation. And then we wonder why we aren't manifesting what we want. Or we begin to see signs that our reality is coming, and the experience becomes a struggle. We start to push for what we think this new experience should look like. We push and struggle, and then the experience fizzles. Nothing happens, and we become very disappointed.

Anytime we feel that we have to force something to happen, we are not working from within creation. We are working at it. When we do this, we are not working with truth. Instead, we are mentally provoking chaos because the messages we are sending out are very mixed. What we mean to create just can't happen because we didn't give clear enough instructions.

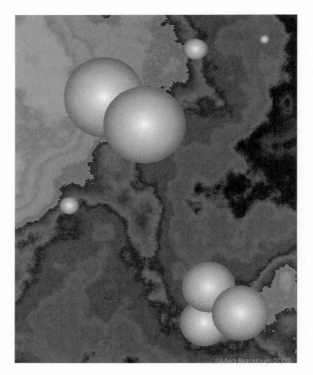

When we send out our intention with doubts and fears, we send a fragmented message to creation (graphic by author)

When we become focused upon what might happen or what could be as a result of any given situation, we are sending our very fears out into creation. When we do, the reality that is created is just what we didn't want. In fact, it's everything that we feared!

What we send out, we get back. It is a rule of natural law. The old saying "what goes around, comes around" couldn't be truer!

In essence and in fact, we are the creators of our realities. Using our consciousness, we can create anything we wish simply by imagining it, by choosing it. As we project an imagined reality outward into creation, our intention communicates through the corridors of creation, and the intention, therefore, becomes a reality. If we believe in the reality, it must be so. In other words, since we have imagined a new reality and sent the message out, our imagined reality becomes a creation of our intention. By our imagining, the reality already exists. Now we simply have to do our part so that we and our desired reality intersect in the perfect moment. By our imaginings, we become part of the integral process of the creation of our new experience.

The key to creating reality is to focus on the outcome rather than the process.

It doesn't matter how many times we send our intention of the new reality into creation, because each time we do, we are harmonically different. Our moods are different. Our thoughts are different. If we send our intentions out more than once, we send a different message each time. This is why affirmations, little sentences that we repeat over and over again to empower ourselves, serve to do just the opposite of what we intend. We become dependent upon them and close the door to anything different.

Once is enough—that is, as long as we haven't sent all our doubts and fears along with our intention. When we project our doubts and fears into the equation, or we have expectations of how our new reality will work, we get exactly what we doubt, fear, or expect—nothing more and often less. By our negative thoughts, we literally limit our own powers of creation. Creation has unlimited possibilities from which to draw to bring to us what we request. So it is important to project a clean message that has clear instructions.

When we imagine a new reality and then set it free, trusting that our desire will return to us, we get a wholly different result. We get everything we wanted and more. When we project our new reality into the universe with the belief that it has already occurred, our intention becomes an instant reality. All we have to do is our part. We must be available to make the choices that are necessary to bring about our intended outcome. A good friend of mine calls this praying *and* moving your feet.

Sending our message out into the creative process is a lot like throwing a ball. Imagine that you hold your intention in your hand. Hold your desire to your heart and fuel it with passion. Imagine not the details of how the new reality will be, but instead how you will feel when your reality is so. Breathe that feeling through your body and into the intention you hold in your hand, and then let that intention fly. The message will

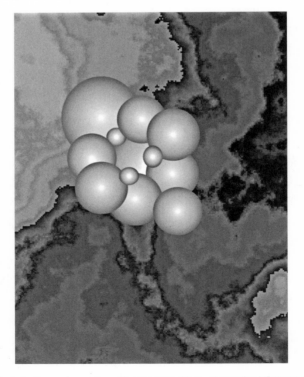

Intent that is fueled with passion and no other thoughts, ideas, or negative influences travels with a clear, strong message for successful manifestation (graphic by author)

travel strongly and clearly into the construct of creation, communicating your intention like a joyful song. As the message travels, creation begins to restructure and make your intention a reality. What you sent out ultimately comes back to you, designed from the infinite possibilities that are available. Your creation has the potential to be far beyond your imaginings because it wasn't limited.

When we project passion along with our intended reality, the passion fuels our request, acting as a propulsive energy that carries our intention far and wide. Passion also gives intensity to the messages that we are sending out, making our requests loud and clear. The information travels with a greater power of speed and clarity, moving faster and further into the creative process and bringing our new reality to us without delays or confusion about what we have commanded. When we send clear, open-ended instructions into the infinite, the results are strong, quick, and full.

This creative process is what makes our prayers work. We have all heard of cases where people prayed fervently for the healing of another person and that person miraculously became well, against all odds. The prayers were projected *with passion* for the healing of the recipient and with the *belief* that a difference could be made. *And so it was.* In these cases, the people who prayed created a new reality through their intentions and passion. They literally *created* the healing through their prayers. The prayers were conscious energy, and they took the message of wellness loudly and clearly to creation.

The bottom line is that we are the creator that we seek.

Our power of creation isn't dependent upon anyone or anything but us. If we believe in our intention, it is already so, and we are on our way to meeting the reality of our creation!

Inciting a Dimensional Shift

If we can change our individual circumstances, can we change our world too? You bet! Remember from Chapter Three how matter manifested in the form of first four-sided pyramids and then later as octahedrons? And that all patterns of creation repeat in the tiniest aspects of creation, as well as in the dimensional construct?

Dimensions are octahedrons. Within each dimension are sets of harmonics that have memories of their source. We are literally part of those sets of harmonics. We are created from organizations of particulates, each of which has consciousness. But more than that, because of how we were formed in relation to all other things, we *are* consciousness. Because each of us exists within our current dimension of reality, we are each one of the tiny aspects of consciousness that create the reality of the whole within our dimension.

What is important is that each of us, as living consciousness, has within us a very special gift. That gift is free will. By the very nature of who we are, we have the power to intentionally direct our will toward a desired outcome. We, as living energy forces within a dimension, can combine and project our free will toward a common goal. When we do, we literally reharmonize the energies within our dimension, causing the dimension to change its relationship to all other dimensions around it.

As our dimension reharmonizes from its interior (us), it will actually rotate in its place and change its harmonic relationship to the rest of creation. When it does, the reality, the experience of living, and even the perceptions of those of us who live here change. Not only do all of these things change, but all reality in every dimension is also affected. We have literally created a new, infinite set of harmonics.

When more than one of us gets together with the same pure intention, the energy of our collective consciousness expands exponentially. Each time we gather with a single intention, the potential for change becomes greater and greater, depending upon the number of us and the purity of our intention.

Multiple studies have monitored events such as mass meditations. These studies have shown that focused intention actually created peaks in the electromagnetic field.

Getting a group of people to all focus on the same intention is a difficult feat, because each and every participant has an idea of how the outcome looks. Instead of focusing on specifics, group consciousness is much more effective when it takes a more general perspective. Remember how we created reality by thinking about how we will feel when we are immersed in our new reality? The same principle works with groups as well.

A group of people can focus on an outcome and project how they will feel when the outcome has been achieved. In this way, creation is getting multiple messages that are harmonized into a hugely powerful tidal wave of energies, all calling for the same outcome. And creation obliges.

The bottom line is that, en masse, we have the power to literally change our reality just by coming together and imagining the change to be so.

Meditation 5

The Power Within

Imagine that you have the power to create whatever change you desire. Consider the possibility that your power does not require aggression. The only responsibility you have is to yourself. The possibilities are unlimited. Where would you start? If your life could be anything that you wanted it to be from this moment forward, what would be different from now?

Chapter Six

The Shift Has Begun:
Interdimensional Events Leading to 2012

We have learned that consciousness is not limited to the third dimension and that there are dimensions of reality infinitely laid out in a pattern of both the above and the below. Above, or outwardly, the harmonics of each dimension become more and more refined until there is only light and a unity of all consciousness. Below, the harmonics of creation become more and more compacted into physical reality and, beyond the physical, denser and denser reality that ultimately leads to a point of creation again. As above, so below; all reality is relative.

Just because most of us can't see, taste, smell, hear, or feel the worlds in other realities doesn't mean they don't exist. Within the worlds of other dimensions, there are amazing beings, different levels of awareness, and even intentions toward universal existence, rather than individual or dualistic consciousness. Each of these realities affects us, whether we realize it or not. As events happen in dimensions outside of our perceived reality, they affect us powerfully.

Unless we are cognizant of the possibility that all dimensions of reality affect us, we probably don't really notice this, except that maybe we feel off balance or our bodies show reactive symptoms. Some of us become irritable, while others feel like crying. These moments can be very powerful, but are usually brief. Sometimes they go on continuously for days or occur off and on for weeks. Our bodies may become overcharged with energy or, conversely, lethargic with aches and pains we can't explain.

Sometimes we experience mild headaches. We might feel as if we can't get enough sleep, or we're so energized that we sleep very little. We may have strange dreams that don't seem to make sense, or in our waking times, we may have quick visions during which we think we just saw something, but can't really say what. The symptoms of interdimensional changes can be vast and varied.

So what kinds of events happen in these other realities? In 2007 and 2009, there were escalations of energy that brought extreme changes to our world. These changes did not signal the approaching end of our world, but the beginning of a new way of being, a new era of reality.

The Arcturian Corridor Opening

The "shift" that many people first in the "New Age" movement and later more commonly have talked about, worked for, and imagined for decades actually began on March 3, 2003, outside of our normal perception, in other-dimensional realms. Even though it occurred in nonlocal reality, this event marked the beginning of us becoming cosmically and energetically "rewired" for the events that are leading up to 2012.

As I mentioned earlier, I first comprehended that beings from other dimensions existed when the Masters began to come into my living room as holograms to teach me wondrous lessons that heightened my awareness and my intelligence and changed forever my perspectives of reality, as well as my values. My lessons progressed beyond the basics to complex theories and applications, transmutation and a plethora of sciences, energy relations, what I call packages of information, and a whole lot more. To the best of my ability I chronicled their words so that I could share them with others and so that I wouldn't forget them in the coming times.

Each time the subject changed, a new Master would appear. When a new one came, I knew that I was in for yet another spectacular ride into the unknown.

After my awareness was sufficiently opened, the Masters began to show me what was happening across the dimensional boundaries and in other realities. These events were not only interdimensional, but also intergalactic, and all of them were interlinked. Further, as I experienced these events, my awareness opened even more, and I began to really understand the intricacies of creation. Nothing could happen anywhere in creation that didn't affect those of us in the third dimension on some level.

On January 16, 2002, I was awakened in the middle of the night with the feeling that someone was watching me—and doing so from very near me. As I startled awake, I beheld a new and different Master standing very close to the edge of my bed.

"I'm dreaming," I thought. But then I sat up and realized that I was wide awake.

This new teacher felt quite commanding, and it was as if he were communicating deep within the construct of my being. I felt him all through me as he made his energy field bigger and bigger to get my attention.

I was a bit aggravated. By that time, I'd learned that these guys just didn't understand that human beings need to sleep, eat, and work, and that we have other physical necessities, too. They often interrupted my sleep, and sometimes it got old. I often became flippant with them, as I did now.

"I'm trying to sleep," I said.

He said nothing.

"Let me sleep!" I said.

He said nothing. His energy just grew more intense.

"*Please* let me sleep!" I pleaded.

The intensity of his energetic "push" became nearly unbearable.

I had also learned that anytime the Masters commanded me or rejected my unwillingness three times in a row, whatever they were trying to share with me was a major truth and whatever was going on would have a perfect outcome, in spite of my reluctance.

"OK, OK . . . ," I grumbled.

Without one further thought, I spontaneously leapt out of my body and was traveling through the cosmos. The new Master was taking me somewhere. Stars ripped by me so fast I couldn't focus on them. Darkness was all around, and I was carried faster than the speed of light through one dimensional reality after another. As I watched, I began to see lines of energy aligning and a corridor opening. It was as if a kaleidoscope of colors and patterns of geometry suddenly came into focus to reveal the most beautiful pathway through creation that I had ever seen. It looked like a tunnel of changing colors of light that were opalescent and phosphorescent. The corridor had an internal rhythm. There was a deep, resonant tone inside. Somehow, the corridor seemed to be *alive*.

Whack! Whack! Whack! The corridor snapped into alignment. The interior became smooth and unobstructed, and there seemed to be no end to its reach through the universe—and beyond, in fact.

"This is the Arcturian Corridor," the Master said. "You are witnessing an event that will occur on March 3, 2003 (3/3/2003) at 3:33 p.m. At this moment, those in your reality will unite to send a message into creation that will open this corridor."

He reminded me that we are the true trinity, saying:

These new energetics are important to the future who you are on all levels. Much of what you receive now are communications that are older than you. You must accept these energies not with your mind, but with your heart of hearts and your soul of souls. When one is operating within the energetics of the trinity, one is also operating within the perfection of that which is held within the energy of the pyramid. In the moment in time when the intent is put forth, the corridor will open considerably. As the corridor opens, through the energy that is released, the communications that you need for greater awareness will come to you easily. For some time now, humanity has felt as if it were waiting for instructions, but didn't understand what it was waiting for. Humanity has seen little to no forward motion because it does not know where it is going. This is the beginning of the instructions you need that will come and make your way clear.

Your energy bodies, as well as your physical bodies, will begin to respond. Your DNA will begin to change how it communicates in tandem with your consciousness. Many of you will receive this information in such a way that it will be unmistakably clear to you. Some of you will become wide open to receiving information directly from creation, while others will begin to awaken to an awareness of a greater reality.

With your intentions, you will reopen the Arcturian Corridor. This will be the first of many events as universal alignments continue to occur toward your year 2012.

You must intend this opening with your heart, not with your mind, but with your very heart and soul. You will send a clear signal into creation that you are able and willing to participate in this event and that you are clear for reception. . . . [Y]ou must send the signal energetically through your heart area [to indicate] that you are awaiting instructions.

For some time now, many of you have been requesting information from higher and higher states of consciousness. You have been heard.

As the corridor opens, you will be encoded with what you have requested. Fully and completely, this encoding will become part of you. The information that you will receive will ignite your particulates into different states of harmonics so that you can experience more awareness than you have previously.

Over the next months, in your way of measuring time, you will be completely reharmonized on a particulate level. That which you are will be that which you become. As the corridor first begins to open, you may feel somewhat unbalanced or unsettled, but that will be brief. During the three months that the corridor remains open, you will have the opportunity to refine that change that occurred within you.

Time: for the most part, the harmonics of energy that will occur upon the opening of the corridor have been inaccessible since before the dawn of humanity, but they have been utilized by a few of your predecessors during times of enlightenment.

There are only certain moments throughout millennia that creation configures and aligns so that this corridor can open. This day and this moment that we speak of is the highest possible distribution of clarity that there has been since humans began to walk the earth. This is the future of what you *are* in relation to all things.

• • •

And so it had officially begun—our journey toward even greater awareness and 2012. I sent this information out to my email list, never dreaming of the effect it would have. At the exact moment of the corridor opening, there were groups of thousands and thousands of people all over the world holding ceremonies, beating drums, meditating, holding space, and even being quiet and still. I was awestruck at how far-reaching the Master's messages had gone and, more so, how people had responded to them. This revelation told me a great deal about the state of consciousness in our world. I learned that *we are ready to embrace a new way of being.* A vital part of the shift had just ignited in the form of human intention coalescing toward a singular outcome.

The Ceylon Star-Gate System Alignment

The next major multidimensional event that prompted a leap in the advancement of human consciousness was the Ceylon star-gate system alignment. The Ceylon (pronounced si-ˈlän) star gate system was driven into an infinite alignment through the corridors of creation by the natural movement and pulsation of the mass of creation.

As the mass of creation pulsates, everything within it moves. Sometimes corridors connecting dimensions, and portals or gateways in and out of certain dimensions, are open and unobstructed. At other times, they are closed. When the movement of the mass of creation returns to a point when the corridors clear and the dimensional doorways are unobstructed, star-gate alignments occur. Star gates are areas within the construct of creation that regulate access to different areas for different reasons. Usually star gates are located between barriers within the space-time continuum.

The Ceylon alignment culminated on September 17, 2007, and the star gates in this system will remain in alignment for a period of seven years. Never before in human history has there been an alignment of such magnitude, opening corridors reaching so far across dimensional barriers.

In the ancient language of light, this kind of shift is called *Lah hanai nu alan nahallah si en tallah ensitu.* Loosely translated, it means: *"The storms within you and around you are leaving so that your remembering of Light can fill you."*

During the Ceylon star-gate shift, we were jerked energetically from one end of creation to another and back again. During the time this shift was occurring, I had countless phone calls and emails in which everyone asked what the heck was going on. Their emotions were running the gamut; others around them were acting out. There were a lot of life changes going on too—people were spontaneously releasing old, withheld emotions; moving house; leaving relationships; changing jobs; changing friends. And no one had a clue why they and others were feeling and acting like they were.

As the Ceylon star-gate system aligned, it created an infinite opening past the void and fully into the heart of the source of all creation. Essentially, what occurred with this vast opening was a merger of past, present, and future in the form of new realities. How those realities shape up depends upon each and every one of us.

The Masters said during this event:

The reason that all of you are affected is that all that has ever been, and all that is, is mirrored within you. Each of you carries light of the highest vibration. The eternal light that can never be extinguished, that light from which all things are made.

Because you are such powerful beings, containing the light of the *is*, everything that you do, every thought that you think, every word that you speak, every action that you create, and every reaction that you have communicates within the One in such a way that the One responds to you.

That shift that you have prayed for, talked about, and worked toward bringing forth, has begun.

Shifting is a process, a shaking out of all that is not true, a bringing forth of greater reality in such a way that your lives, your beingness as humans upon your earth, have the potential to become of the highest vibration that the density of creation has ever achieved. Of course, this is all up to you.

The alignment of the Ceylon star-gate system acts as a clarion call to all of creation to respond in like manner. As the alignment occurs, there is an inherent reaction within all beingness that responds first by releasing that which does not serve the truth and then by polarizing toward either the highest of vibrational existence or that which is opposite. How you choose to step along the path toward utopian existence is up to you.

You and your world are beginning to change. You are at a pivotal point in the existence of humanity. There is, at this time, a struggle for balance, as this *is* and the *has been* battle into new paradigms. That which *has been* no longer has a place that can work in your reality. The guidelines that have been used for discernment, problem solving, and even the creation of reality no longer work because harmonically, it is impossible to live what is not truth.

Imagine allowing yourself to ride the tide of higher nature, letting go of the resistance and being carried easily and with grace into greater reality.

As the shifting occurs and the changes begin, many of you are finding that the world around you, your daily experiences, and even those experiences of the moment are fraught with changing values that are in direct conflict with those [values] that you have carried forth unto this now. Those values have told you that to have and to hold are that for which you exist. Those values have told you that you must become outstanding above all others, to achieve beyond others, to be special in your presentation to the world.

Those old values simply are not Truth. They belie all that you are and all that you can be in Truth.

We speak of intentional participation within the reality of all things for the greater good of the balance and the coalescence of individualized reality into one greater experience—the experience of being one with joy and ease, with regard to and honor for everyone who is doing the very best that they know how to do, in every given moment, to participate within their journeys, as are you.

Some beings involved in the natural process of all change will not choose to step out into the unknown, greater state of being. Do not grieve for them. You must know that, first of all, change is a choice, and secondly, they will have other opportunities to rise to their greater beingness. Do not fear; do not be concerned. All is perfection in each moment. Live your truth and walk your talk. The time is now.

As the Ceylon star-gate system brings focused source energy to your beingness, to your planet, you will find that not only are the veils thinning, but you will also experience dimensional overlaps. What this means is that the reality to which you are accustomed and that exists in other dimensions will occasionally overlap, blurring the lines between both realities so that they become of one reality temporarily.

You may find yourselves wondering what is real and what is imagined. We tell you this: *it is all real.*

There are portals opening that you may use for multilevel experience. You already exist within all realms of reality simultaneously. You can become conscious of this and other realities simultaneously simply by aligning all of your aspects (by intention) in the same manner that the star gates aligned. As you do this deliberately, you have begun to live purposely, accepting balance within your existence and participating consciously from within the One. This is how you create conscious reality.

You cannot do this from your thinking self; you must align from your core, your three-fold flame, your heart of hearts. It is there that your inherent knowing resides. It is there that the vault of all knowing has been hidden from you. No one has deliberately hidden your knowing; you have simply become unaware that it exists within you due to evolutional processes. You needed to learn to communicate as you evolved, so later you developed both the thinking self and the ego self. As both of these progressed, emotionality fragmented into a plethora of subtleties that became known as love, hate, fear, grief, happiness, and so on.

Each emotion was just a part of a greater whole that you could not see, because as each of these traits developed individually, yet worked collectively, you began to think that you were and are individuals. With the newly evolved perceptions of self, doors to greater awareness closed, and that is where the illusion began. That is where the lies of separation were launched.

But deep within you, the truth remained. You do not need to discover the memories, the rememberings, by searching for halls of records that are buried in ancient lands (although they are there). You do not need to become an initiate of a school or a form of thought or a system of learning. You have all that you need and all that has ever been within you. Let yourself ride the current of blissful existence, for as you let go of that which was, and do not worry about that which might be, that which you are responds to the freedom of the moment and does not simply fly, but begins to soar.

Physically, the electromagnetic fields within and around your DNA strands are changing. These fields of energy act as transmitters and receivers within you and outside of you in universal proportions. Infinite proportions. It is these electromagnetic fields that bring information to you in each and every moment, telling you what options are available and what doors are open or closed to you, based upon the choices you have made up to this now.

The DNA fields are reharmonizing. Many of you have talked about, read, or heard about twelve-strand DNA. Of course, this is not exactly accurate. The phrase "twelve-strand DNA" refers to multidimensional aspects of the physical and the harmonization of them as a singular and functional unit of matter. Further, applying a count of your strands implies that you are not infinite. Of course, you are infinite. What we are saying to you is that your little, tiny electromagnetic energy fields are responding to the opening of the Ceylon star-gate system.

As the star gates align and open, your DNA fields respond. As they do, an amazing thing happens: the harmonization of the electromagnetic DNA fields creates harmonic resonance in the form of a single active field that reaches infinitely to the highest of highs and the depths of the most base energies. You are becoming infinitely balanced, not only as part of the One, but also as the One.

Do you understand what this means? This means that you, as insignificant as you have seen yourself in the scheme of things, as lacking in value as you may have seen yourself, are becoming mightily powerful, more so in each moment that passes, as you and the star gates are one and the same.

From your universal harmonic resonance, there is nothing you can't create. There is nothing you can't do. Everything that you ever dreamed of is only a perception away. How is it that you see yourself? How is it that you view your world? Whatever your answer is, that is your truth. In order to change your truth, stop seeing with the eyes of others; reach way down deep within yourself, and look through your infinite eyes. They do not lie. There is no ego within them. Your infinite eyes draw from the source of your being, the source of all things, and know unfailingly of the greatness, the purity, and the scope of infinite love that is you—that has always been you.

As the star-gate system aligns and opens, there is a universal response that occurs. All of creation begins to shift and respond much in the same way as your DNA fields respond. All of creation is aligning harmonically, based upon the level of reality and the reality within that level. What we are saying to you in this moment is that whatever reality you create is being responded to by all else in creation. This is how your choices become the most powerful of all. The power is in the choosing. What you create here and now is being transmitted to and responded to by all of creation. It is in this manner that you change the existence you are in now to a more utopian existence—the fifth world, beyond the fifth dimension, beyond imagining.

At the same time, your planet, your world, is responding as well. Your planet has begun to expel the pressure of untruth from within its very bowels. This is so as volcanic eruptions occur, as earthquakes begin to shift the balance not only on the surface of the planet, but also within its heart of hearts as well. The planet will continue to do so, and as the star-gate alignment progresses, you will see more anomalous occurrences within the weather patterns, seismic activity, and volcanic eruptions, and even in the behaviors of the peoples upon the planet.

The animals are already beginning to respond by changing their migratory patterns. They are responding by behaving in unexpected ways. And those that have always been loners are beginning to see the value of living and working together, as many of you will begin to see as well. The animals always respond before humanity because they have no mental process to tell them they are wrong. They just do what they feel. Learn from them.

As the universal harmonization takes place, there is another fascinating and wonderful opportunity. Pathways of travel that have not been open since the star nations came to your planet are reopening. Some of you call these wormholes. They are pathways of travel that intersect within all of the star sectors, all of the multidimensional realities, star patternings of pathways—each and all of which culminate in portals in various locations throughout reality.

There are many of the portals that enter into your world. These portals may be used for conscious coming and going to any and all destinations. Do you realize what this means?

Your consciousness is not limited to your body. It is your essence, free and light. Your consciousness can easily traverse these and all other portals to take you into the infinite intentionally and instantly. As your consciousness travels outside of time and space, it is not limited by perceptions, boundaries, or destinations. Your consciousness travels faster than the speed of light, and because it is light, your consciousness remembers everything that it has ever experienced. Imagine allowing yourselves the freedom to glide through all of reality just because you desire and intend to do so. You can bring to your now, your planet, and your current reality whatever and however much you choose.

At the same time, you can intentionally experience multidimensionality, consciously being aware of all other realities simultaneously, and still be functional in the dimension of the third.

It is in this manner that you become aware of how to command the miracles and magic in every moment. That which you intentionally project into all of creation instantaneously responds as a new reality. All that you must do to achieve the magic, to live the miracles, is believe in them. And why not? You are everything that ever was and is now, wrapped up into a perfect representation of beingness in this now!

There are many children coming into your world who come with knowledge and remembering of the before times. Many of them will step out as teachers of the ancient rememberings. They will remind humanity of its perfection. They will demonstrate abilities that until now have only been of the imagination of your science-fiction writers. Let it be so. The children know what they are doing. Do not worship them or, conversely, let them run amok, because even though they carry the rememberings and the apparent giftedness of all time, they are still fragile little beings who have needs. They need guidance within your world, as they are sensitive in nature. Let the children guide you back to your innocence and into the Light. They remember the way home.

In the coming times, you will witness and perhaps even experience much change in your reality and your life. So be it. There is no reason to fear. What is has always been. What is, is. The question is, what will you do in each and every moment?

The world scene will escalate as violence makes an attempt at being that which is the outcome. We tell you that the violence is only a part of the process. Creating reality is not to focus on the process, but rather to know, to believe, that the outcome has already occurred. As this is so, then the violence will become peace, and there will form alliances for the greater good of humanity. What is the greater good of humanity? That is for you, each of you, to contribute to and decide.

You are the denizens of reality. That which you are, you are infinitely. Perhaps elsewhere in creation you have a different face, different frequencies, different journeys, but you are infinitely present.

As the Ceylon star-gate system brings forth the truth of you, and as the space-time continuum begins to overlap, bringing in new and different realities to your awareness, do not hesitate to experience them. Do not fear for your sanity. Your sanity is, after all, only a perception, which is of limited scope [because it is] based upon what you have been taught is acceptable.

Imagine if you never had to worry again about what is acceptable or what the consequences might be. Imagine if you accepted your freedom with grace and ease, living the Truth at any given moment. Even when that truth is, perhaps, unfamiliar, you would find that the Truth is entirely of perfection. Because of this, you would also recognize the perfection of you.

As you begin to witness and experience the coming change, do not hide from yourself and others. Stand in your spiritual might and be among the counted, those who chose the higher road. Reach out and touch your fellow beings, offer your strength, your wisdom, courage, and power, and remind them of theirs. Empower each other and embrace the infinite. You are that might. You are that great power; you are the gentle love that resides in all things. You are the balance. It is only for the choosing.

Many of you we shall meet within the light as you choose to travel intentionally within the open star-gate system. Greet us on equal terms, for each of you is a Master of greatness.

• • •

And here we were thinking that we were nothing more than lowly humans who led limited lives! Humph!

So we begin to see a pattern of unfolding that, even though we aren't necessarily consciously aware of it, affects us deeply. Without realizing it, we are regaining access to greater consciousness and awareness, as well as a reconnection with our divine selves. But it doesn't stop there.

Interdimensional Triangulations

Beginning in June of 2008, we moved through a series of interdimensional triangulations, which harmonically interconnected multiple realities—kind of like when notes on a keyboard come together to make a harmonic chord. This connection not only affected us energetically, but also affected our abilities to move toward higher consciousness.

The intensity of each event was heightened as we continued to move farther and farther toward the galactic center and, therefore, began closing in on the photon belt. Remember from Chapter Three how matter was created from the light within the source as it condensed into dense matter, and how from our reality matter and density became darker and darker until there was again light? Well, our galaxy is put together similarly. As our solar system naturally moves full circle toward its center of beginning, there is a band of light. At the very center point, there is a black hole, which drains off excess pressure in our known universe. On the other side of the black hole is another, parallel reality and more light. We will talk more about this phenomenon in the next section of this chapter.

As the intensity of these powerful interdimensional events progressed, different parts of us were greatly affected. Systematically and progressively, the mental, emotional, physical, and other aspects of our being were shaken to the core. During this time, great numbers of people made serious life changes in the forms of new careers, relationships, even where they lived. Nothing that was untrue could be held inside of us without great pain of some kind.

Again, the Masters provided a full description not only of the event, but also of its effects upon us:

As you approach your galactic center, more and more interdimensional events will take their courses to create natural balance and, in some cases, attune reality so that it remains harmonically resonant with the changes of the coming times.

In this and the coming time, you have entered into cosmic reconstruction of your reality. The very fabric of which you are created is being rewoven. What was the harmonic arrangement of particulates that created the harmonic resonance of you and all other things together is being rewritten as a symphony of change.

Your new particulate arrangements began to occur in the week preceding June 6, 2008, in such a way that the arrangement of particulates experienced a vacuum effect, which is caused by the triangulations of astrological bodies. The triangulations began on the outer edge of the constellation Lira and reached across multiple dimensions for triangulation with Indiron B and Lechtalli, two distant stars in a universe just parallel to your third dimension.

The triangulations continued for about eighteen months. During the process, each new triangulation rotated in sums of degrees that were all divisible by fifteen. This is because the natural pattern of dimensional angulation is always divisible by fifteen degrees. Knowing this, and realizing that interdimensional pathways are always on angulations divisible by fifteen degrees, brings the realization that the very harmonics of which you are made are being reconstructed.

Your particulates, except when excited, are generally aligned by opposition of polarity by increments of thirds. As the series of seven alignments and the transition of one angulation to another occurred, your particulates, the very particles of which you are created, responded. They realigned into other mathematical relations. In other words, the spacing between your very particulates changed. Because of this, you may have experienced unconscious agitation or the feeling that something huge was about to happen. You may have felt that you were having difficulty being grounded and even, at times, disassociated with your everyday world.

This series of events was literally a dimensional shift, for as the triangulations' influences reached you and your reality, both you and your reality were pulled upward in a vacuum effect, much like you would experience during an extreme tidal pull. The difference is that a tidal pull only affects you and your planet. The pull of the triangulations was transdimensional, literally reaching across all realities.

As the pulling began, you may have felt moments of lacking focus or clarity. We tell you that you need not understand what happened, just know that it did. You may have felt at times the sensation that your feet were not on the ground or felt as if you were free-floating, not connected to your body or your earth. The new configuration of your particulates contributes to expand your awareness of realities beyond the mundane. Breathe deeply and intentionally, allowing yourselves to be cleansed of the old, welcoming the new. Your breath is more than that which sustains life. It is a natural cleansing, regenerative, nurturing, and healing tool for living.

Intuitive awareness may have snuck into some of the aspects of being for those who requested to "see" or experience other worlds. Your time has begun. As it has, remember that your journey is your journey. You are always in control. Your experience can be changed or stopped at any time virtually by changing your perception. Remember that it is your experience, and therefore, you are its creator!

About midway through the seven triangulations, there was a series of lateral phenomena that occurred simultaneously. This was a series of geometric configurations that, for about six weeks, brought some stabilization to the effects of each triangulation. There were three of them. And so with the number of seven triangulations and three lateral alignments, came the numbers of man and God to be combined as one.

What we are saying is that the sequence of trinity alignments became a true reharmonization to the perfection of harmonic resonance throughout creation. Whenever there is a new harmonization or even a minor attunement, consciousness is affected, as are your harmonic relationships with everything. In a way, you have been freed from all that has bound you. Because of this, the possibilities for change in your world are infinite and available to you.

This series of events changed the political climate across your globe. Elections had drastic outcomes toward change in many countries. Some international leaders began to understand the need toward common goals for the good of the world, while others escalated even further into even more and desperate destructive behaviors. Untruths surfaced with a command for consequences. Monetary values continued to shift toward changing balance, and at the same time, that which you value also changed.

Also as a result of the pulling effect of the triangulations, there were large seismic activities and the opening of new volcanic vents, particularly off the west coast of the USA. There will be one large volcanic vent opening under the water, as many as three secondary vents spilling lava onto the sea floor, and further shaking in Sumatra and Indonesia, as well as on the New Zealand fault lines.

The coming times will bring great change to your world and your experience of it. What we say to you in this now is that you must remain present, aware of synchronicities that will lead you to where it is that your soul wishes to be. That may be geographically or simply emotionally or experientially. Whatever the course of your journey, truth will command. That which is and has been the mundane will shift in importance. And that is a catalyst to change. What you intend now will manifest purely and completely. Take the time to become aware of your interior. Is your experience that which is in your outer world? Is your experience of balance, and does it bring you joy? If not, now is the time to regroup. Let go of your fears. You are whole, perfect, magnificent creatures of the One. There is no need for you to struggle through your life journey. On the contrary, use these transitional events to bring yourselves to greatness not to anyone but yourselves. When you do this, all is great and all is perfection.

The sense of imperfection or having to heal or change one's self is all part of the illusion that you have created to feel safe. Instead of feeling safe, you find yourselves struggling through your days. What if you truly understood that the struggle is not truth, but that the struggle is merely created by perception? What if you realized that all is perfection? Perfection does not need to be healed or "let go." It merely needs to be acknowledged. When one accepts ones' self and agrees to live one's journey unobstructed by preconceived expectations or beliefs, magic beings, purity of communication universally begins. Life begins.

We have spoken with you previously about the universal construct. We have explained to you how the geometries of light arranged in pyramid form, then in octahedronal format, to create the fabric of all creation. All of the inherent geometry is created by light harmonized. All of that light carries consciousness. You are that. You are created of the very light of creation. And within you are the memories. You are an enfoldment of all time and all things, manifested to feel, experience, touch, hold, and even to release all that you encounter. From one moment to the next, there is only ever this now. Do not miss the glorious possibilities that are available to you by living outside of yourselves. Reach inward—deeply, honestly. Who is hiding there? What will it take for you to come out and become the experience you seek? There is nothing you cannot do.

There are times when chaos leads to magnificence; in fact, all chaos has the potential for magnificence. Chaos is a direct catalyst for change. Without it, you would become complacent, too comfortable in your discomfort. Embrace the chaos as one of the finest tools for change. Let yourselves be carried in the current of the now. Now is the time. Greet the light as it washes you clean each morning. Embrace the following darkness as a time for regeneration. And in the moments of the dawn, when it is neither light nor dark, be still and listen. You are being called to greatness. Are you listening?

The final triangulation on June 11, 2009, harmonically unified the universal field in such a way that a series of dimensional shifts became possible and, in fact, probable. When dimensional shifts happen, there also comes a change in perception and reality. The fullness of each shift, as well as its outcome, is entirely dependent upon the reactivity of those within that reality.

When there is consciousness of acceptance and, in fact, co-creation, the shifting is easy and full in nature. When there is consciousness of resistance, the shifting can be chaotic and less effective.

In your current world there exists a blending of both aspects of consciousness due more to ignorance than to true diversion. As each of you takes responsibility for simply being who you are, you begin to unify your consciousness away from duality and back toward your true sense of divinity. At that moment, you are one step closer to a complete shift in reality and, therefore, experience.

You are recreating the human experience and contributing to the infinite experience of all realities. Bring to your creation the beauty that is within you.

• • •

Every aspect of our being was addressed energetically with the triangulation events. We received a cosmic rewiring, a cleansing of great proportion. Even though we may have looked the same, we had become very different in our harmonic relations to each other and to all of creation. Many of us began to see the world a little differently, and from there the interdimensional activity escalated even further.

Spontaneous Opening of Star Gates and Wormholes

On October 3, 2009, the most intensive series of multidimensional and interdimensional events to date began. This series of events was an immense and rapid opening of a series of star-gate systems that began to unify wormhole systems both intergalactically and into parallel realities. This sequence of events was the beginning of a domino effect, as one star gate, then the corridor, then the matrix of corridors, then others opened. These events continue even today as we race toward—and beyond—2012.

As discussed earlier in the chapter, star gates, areas within creation that regulate access to different areas, are usually located between barriers within the space-time continuum. As creation pulses and moves, there are times when the star gates cannot possibly open because they are blocked by part of the mass of creation. At other times, when things line up perfectly, these systems will spontaneously open.

Wormholes are tunnels that connect one star gate to the next. Wormholes thread through bends in the space-time continuum, connecting one reality or frequency level of creation to another. They may network to connect series of star gates, like the Ceylon star-gate system discussed at the beginning of this chapter. In the wormhole systems are intersections where one can change direction and move from one star constellation, dimension, parallel, or reality to another. Within this wormhole network, there are also portals that serve as secondary gates through which one can pop into another reality. In ancient times before our recorded history, the Lemurians and other peoples traveling from parallel realities used the wormhole systems to travel to earth. There were multiple entry points on the planet, including ancient Egypt, Atlantis, Antarctica, Mexico, and others. The system that made planet earth accessible is about to open again.

Moving within a wormhole is done one of three ways. The first is on a particulate level, with a disassembly of mass. This is kind of a "Beam me up, Scotty" technique, but far more ancient and advanced.

Another way to move through wormholes is inside of a specific geometric form, such as a spaceship or energy form that has the appropriate electromagnetic polarities and the ability to adjust those polarities as one switches from one density of reality to another. (I feel that perhaps the Vimana of ancient India are crafts that move this way, and they may be coming into and out of our reality.) As one moves from one level of creation to another, the densities vary, and the electromagnetic fields must be adjusted (or set to adjust automatically) so flux rates and oscillation can ensure a successful journey. Failure to maintain these constant fluctuations results in a complete and permanent disassembly of one's particulates.

The third way to travel in the corridors of the wormhole system is consciously. One can project their consciousness into the system and travel to destinations across creation. In doing so, one can meet and interact with beings that exist in far-away realities, planets, and universes—and beyond.

(When we become adept with this kind of travel we can actually share those travels in tandem with other people. I have several friends with whom I can "piggyback" consciousness to travel the wormhole systems. We all see and experience the exact same things when we do.)

When the Masters spoke to me of these events, when the system of star gates and wormholes began to spontaneously align and then open, they well described the process and its effects on us. In the visions they showed me, the star gates and wormholes were like rivers and tributaries, all interconnected and gaining a momentum of flow. As the flow of openings progressed, more and more branches came to light. The Masters said:

> There are many events that will escalate in the coming times.
> Now that the triangulations have culminated and particulate
> relationships are reordered and reharmonized, there comes a vast
> opening of multiple star-gate systems. This is a multilevel system,
> meaning that it crosses the time-space continuum and dimensional
> thresholds and is interconnected by a vast series of wormhole
> systems. These systems are regulated with something that resembles
> a valve system, which allows, for lack of a better description in your
> language, for a vacuum-system type of operation, which in turn
> allows for the expedient transfer of matter in particulate form.
> At the same time, these valves, which are the star gates, maintain
> positive and negative pressure thresholds between transfer stations
> and angulation changes within the system.
>
> This series of star-gate systems was utilized by the precursors of the
> Atlanteans, who were beings of an intergalactic nature. These systems
> are the Um, the Lenhe, the Aetnalin, the Urnallum, the Renari, the
> Leioni, and the Dendor. Seven systems—the number of truth.
>
> This [opening of the star-gate systems] began on the third of
> October, 2009.
>
> The combination of star-gate systems opening and astronomical
> events will bring to your world evidence of visitors from other worlds,
> because your world will once again be accessible to distant travelers.

One area of this system remained open during the times of ancient Egypt, and it opened into subterranean chambers. The system closed in 624 BC and has not been operational since then. It will soon be again.

As the openings occur, there will be a certain amount of dimensional bleed-through. Some of you will see or hear beings of other realities as these brief bleed-throughs happen. It is nothing but energy, memory contained within light, and there is nothing to fear. At the same time, energies will blur the lines of division and cross into your dimension in such a way that there may be brief and intense changes, such as when the wind changes direction before the weather changes. These events you will feel inside of you as if something light has just walked across your inside.

Know that the sacred sites that are built at specific intervals upon your planet are amping up to a frequency response in answer to the cosmic changes. It is vital to know that the new frequencies are acting as portals to the infinite and that these sites are in the process of harmonizing. There will be further events in this regard.

Know that events from now forward in the coming few years will escalate, and intensity will occur in and around you at times. If you do not resist, your experiences will be of an extremely positive nature. There will be a seven-month period in which the energies will flow in such a positive form and frequency that your vibrational escalation can leap and arc into higher and more intricate frequency sets without some of the usual steps in escalation being necessary. In other words, your frequencies—your vibrations, as you call them—can rise uninhibited, and your experiences will be a leap of escalation of your very being in relation to all other things.

You must know that you have requested of the Universe a great shift that would change your world. It [the shift] is so, and it has begun. You must also know that there is never change without chaos.

Consider whatever chaos you encounter to be a grand sign that the shifting is moving into full swing. To ease the way during these times, do not be reactive, but instead focused and living intentionally. Be of care in what you intend, as it will be so, and that reality will contain the doubts and fears that you sent with your message of creation.

Create from your heart of hearts in such a way that you bring to your experience only that which you truly desire. Do not focus on what was, because it is lost in the changes. Know that what is now is all that matters.

Know that you have chosen optimal times to occupy human form and to experience a vast depth of awareness, emotion, and physicality. You are part of a greater happening that is eons in coming and infinite in its reach—as are you.

• • •

We are in for one heck of a ride as events outside of our reality escalate. When interdimensional events occur, we may experience any number of symptoms. Many have reported new awareness, including seeing new energy patterns, colors, and geometries and feeling harmonic integrations of their energy systems. Others report symptoms such as hyperactivity and excess energy, or the opposite—lethargy and lack of motivation. On an emotional level, great emotional releases have been taking place. A lot of tears have been shed, and internal freedom from the baggage of past experience is being embraced.

Intolerance for untruth has been escalating big time. If it doesn't ring true, more and more people are no longer willing to accept the status quo. This intolerance has affected every aspect of living. Those experiencing these effects are likely to have decided that their long- or short-term relationships no longer fit, or they realize that the relationships are based upon lack of truth. These relationships are ending fast. Further, people are changing jobs and careers as they wake up to the fact that they aren't living to work, but working to live, and so they may as well be happy while working. People are on the move, too, suddenly having intense urges to relocate to places they haven't ever been. Locations on the planet are harmonized, just as we are, so after we change, we often feel that we must change our place or area of living as well.

One aspect of the shift that I most love is that people are coming out of their spiritual closets and beginning to live their truth—whatever that looks like to them—openly. When we live our truths, we teach by example. We also exchange the energy of our experience with everyone around us. And yes, the energy is contagious, but in a great way.

As we race toward 2012, we will experience more and more internal and external change. The greatest difficulty during any period of change occurs when we resist. When we resist, we clamp down our subtle energies and become denser, making it difficult for creation to maintain our attunement along the way. When we can relax into the changes and be willing to accept new and different possibilities in our experiences, things flow much easier, and we are infinitely more comfortable all the way around.

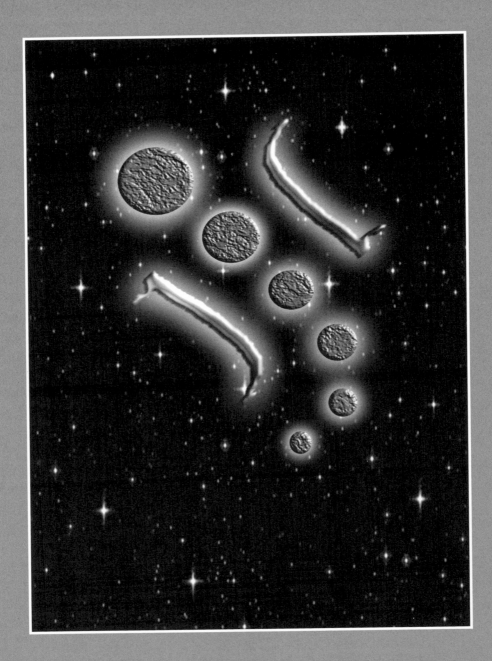

Meditation 6

Continuity

Imagine that you are a thread in the tapestry of creation. Who you are and what you do is intricately related to all other things, no matter how large or small. Imagine that everything that you contribute in the way of actions, words, thoughts, feelings, and beliefs—*everything*—has an infinite effect on everything else in creation. How can you begin to live intentionally, so that your contribution to creation has positive outcomes?

Chapter Seven

Changing Consciousness:
2012 and How We Are Affected

Coming Full Circle

Throughout this book, we have discussed consciousness and how a map for us was laid out in sacred sites all over the globe by our ancient predecessors. We have learned how we can experience higher awareness. Past and present have come together in a moment of truth. That truth is that there is only ever this now, yet this now is infinitely and indelibly linked to our past and to our future. Consciousness is infinite and indivisible.

As consciousness continues to evolve, events are shaping up toward a moment in time that many say will be the end of time as we know it. Doomsayers claim that the end of days, that the absolute end of the world is fast approaching. It is not.

Some inherent memory in our psyches challenges humanity to predict its own demise with fear and trepidation and even a little unacknowledged excitement. There have been events in our past that literally wiped out entire civilizations to the point that we don't even know who they were or any of their history. The light in our bodies remembers all of these events—because it remembers everything—but we don't consciously recall those events. So with that nagging sense of our indefinable memories in the background, we speculate that the world may end again soon. Great tales are woven about times past and deeds done, and yet something inside of us has a vague fear that those catastrophic events humanity experienced in the past will happen again.

The truth is that much of our future is up to us. Our future depends on how we live, how expanded we allow our consciousness to become, how we treat our planet, and what we do with the technologies that we have. We can create a greater world, or we can be the incubus of our destruction. Remember, as we discussed earlier, all energy travels and communicates within creation and brings new realities to us. What we put out we *will* get back. This is a universal law that is inescapable. What is it that we want? What future are we creating in this now?

The coming of 2012 is just one more opportunity for us to speculate endlessly about the so-called imminent end of humanity. There is always a stimulus for our fear. In the year 2000, it was Y2K, when we thought the world would fall apart because our computers weren't programmed to change millennial dates. Now, as we approach 2012, there are books and movies out the wazoo that tell us the world is ending and that we should be terrified. People are hoarding food and supplies, and men, women and children are scared out of their wits. This fear is a very sad and unnecessary thing.

Our current perception is predicated by our lack of complete understanding of a set of calendars that were left to us by the ancient Mayans. Instead of a doomsday perspective, let's look at a fresh point of view on this subject.

The True Meaning of the Mayan Calendar

In order to understand what the big deal is about the Mayan calendar, we must first have at least a basic idea of what it is and how it works. The Mayan calendar is actually not one calendar, but many, and they operate as intricately woven keepers of time, traditions, planetary movement, and even periods of consciousness and human evolution. The composite calendar tracks time and humanity, planets and solar systems, galaxies, and universes. It measures every detail of our solar system's movement as the planets, and we, travel for nearly 26,000 years, from the galactic center of our beginning and then return, full circle, back to the galactic center. This calendar is a marvel of accomplishment by any standard, but particularly since, at the time it was written, there were no telescopes, no computers—in fact, no technology whatsoever—for the Mayans to have calculated this intricate system. The calendar even includes celestial bodies that aren't visible to the naked eye. But the calendar is unerring!

The Mayan calendar began on day 0.0.0.0.0, on the eleventh of August in the year 3114 BC. The calendar is said to end at exactly 11:11 a.m. GMT, on December 21, 2012 (day 13.0.0.0.0 in what is known in the calendar as the Long Count). This moment in time represents an extremely close conjunction of the winter solstice sun with the crossing point of the galactic equator (the equator of the Milky Way) and the ecliptic (the path of the sun). The ancient Maya recognized this moment of alignment as the Sacred Tree. This event has been moving into harmonic resonance slowly, but surely, for nearly 26,000 years.

Scholars and hobbyists alike have claimed that the Mayan calendar is based upon a series of harmonics that at certain points in time resonate toward different realities and meanings. Simply stated, the calendar series is composed of:

The Tzolkin: A harmonic of the Great Cycle, this calendar can be used to track history. It is a 260-day calendar based upon the period of human gestation. It is comprised of twenty-day signs, each of which has thirteen variations, which were used to determine character traits and time harmonics, much like our astrology wheel is used today. Loosely translated, the day-sign glyphs can be interpreted as:

1.	Alligator	Death	Monkey	Owl
2.	Wind	Deer	Grass	Quake
3.	House	Rabbit	Reed	Knife
4.	Lizard	Water	Jaguar	Rain
5	Serpent	Dog	Eagle	Flower

The Haab: A 365-day calendar in which we start to see the mythological uses of the sacred calendar. The quality of a year is determined by which day sign falls on New Year's Day, the first day of the Haab.

The Venus: A 584-day cycle based upon the fact that Venus rises as the morning star approximately every 584 days. This was an important cycle to the Maya, because they tracked the movements of the sun and Venus very closely. There is some speculation that the Tzolkin arose, at least in part, to give structure to the related cycles of the sun and Venus. The relationship between the solar and Venus cycles is quite simple: five Venus cycles equals eight Haab. The influence of a third extraterrestrial factor, the earth's moon, was also built into the Tzolkin cycle. The movement of Venus traces a five-pointed star in the sky over a period of eight years. The eight-year transit is representative of the musical octave. The musical octave contains eight notes, a basic set of harmonics, with implied overtones that aren't actually notes, but tones that are made by the playing of notes in the scale. These implied notes, in conjunction with those actually played, create *harmonic resonance*. So the cycle of Venus weaves a full scale of harmonic frequencies through the rest of the calendar.

The Long Count: A calendar that tracked long periods of time. It consists of all of the other parts of the main calendar, plus the following subcalendars:

> **Tun:** One 360-day year, which consists of eighteen twenty-day months (Uinals).
>
> **Katun:** Twenty Tuns.
>
> **Baktun:** Nearly 400 years.

Great Cycle: 1,872,000 days (5,200 Tuns, or about 5,125 years).

The Grand Year: 26,000 Tuns, or five great cycles (or progressions of equinoxes).

At the moment of the culmination of the Mayan calendar, all of the cycles reach their end point at the same time, and full harmonic resonance occurs. There is no indication that the calendar goes one moment forward from this point. Many interpret this abrupt ending of the calendar as the end of the world, a time when great earth changes will shake us into oblivion, or a huge asteroid will completely wipe out us little ol' folks on earth, or some other unimaginable catastrophe will take us out of existence. This isn't necessarily the real story!

A New Perspective

Let's take a different perspective on the magnificent march of our solar system and what it really means to us. It is my greatest sense that if we could see the Mayan calendar in action as it progressed from beginning to end, with all its respective aspects in a moving form, we would see that the combined motion of all its parts would intertwine until they presented a singular holographic image in the form of a torus tube.

The torus is a self-contained, never-ending form of the infinite. It is considered to be a perfect form of geometry and often occurs in nature. It has no clear beginning or end and is perfect in its harmonics and balance. The torus is a portal, a gateway, to infinite consciousness. It is based upon electromagnetic polarities that, under certain conditions, can reverse. The toroid is found everywhere in the formation of our known reality:

The torus tube, a perfect form of the space-time continuum and of the flow of energy universally

- Our universe is a toroid of energy.

- Our solar system emits a toroid of energy.

- The earth's core has a toroidal field of geomagnetic energy. This intense field is subject to polarity changes that can literally reverse our magnetic poles from north-south to south-north in an instant.

- The black hole at the center of our universe is a huge toroid shape, and it functions like the center of a torus as well. In the torus, everything flows in a repetitive pattern toward the central portal. The same movement occurs in black holes that are thought to "eat" stars and planets. All of these black holes act as balancing points between one universe and parallel universes. The sum of all of these universes that are linked by torus fields of energy is called the multiverse. We also refer to the multiverse as creation.

- Our sun moves in a toroid pattern. (Given this movement, the ancient worship of the sun as the giver of all light is significant.)

- Our galactic center is a toroid. As the precession of our solar system rotates in its constant pattern, which is predicted in the Mayan calendar, the electromagnetic energies fluctuate within a toroid pattern, causing ebbs and flows of electromagnetic energies and harmonics. Because our consciousness is created of the same kind of energy, periods of expanded and contracted consciousness occur, as well as harmony and disharmony. Expanded awareness and darkness occur, depending upon the harmonics. *In other words, states of consciousness on all levels of existence are cyclic and predictable!*

The Sacred Geometrical Sense of It All

But how does the toroid apply to us? In order to get a grip on this idea, let's start at the beginning and see the torus process in its formation.

In sacred geometry, a basic principle is that all creation is defined by a circle, and within the very center of that circle is a defining point that represents the source of all creation—the divine.

In other words, all actions within creation bounce off the interior walls of the circle and at some point meet the divine.

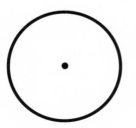

Basic geometric illustration of creation

Within this principle is the implied theory that everything that happens does so as it interacts between the outer circle and the

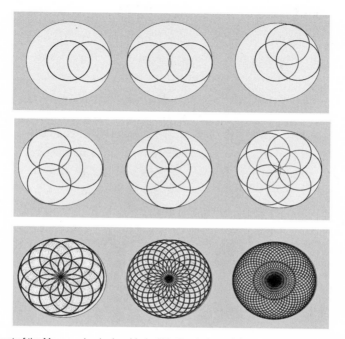

As each part of the Mayan calendar is added within the circle, and the movement of each calendar is interwoven with the others, the geometry culminates in a torus tube. Note that during the process, the sixth figure from the left is the Flower of Life, seen in sacred sites all over the world! I contend that the Flower of Life represents the six major aspects of the Mayan calendar. (Graphic by author)

divine core in the center. The outer circle and divine core are synonymous in their existence. One does not exist without the other. The circle with the dot in the center can also be interpreted as representing the relationship between humanity (the outside circle) and our source, the divine (the middle dot).

As its varied sections weave together within the form of the circle, the Mayan calendar illustrates different cycles of harmonics in measured time. All of the calendar sections interact with all of the subcalendars as part of the Long Count that culminates the Great Cycle. From the fullness of the Great Cycle, the measurement tracks ultimately to a perfect geometric form in a moment in time called the Grand Year. The current Grand Year is 2012.

From the beginning of the Mayan calendar on day 0.0.0.0.0, on August 11 in the year 3114 BC, to the end date of the calendar (day

13.0.0.0.0) at exactly 11:11 a.m. GMT on December 21, 2012, a lot of cyclic movement will have taken place. The interwoven movements of the totality of the Mayan calendar take the basic circle principle of creation into the torus, a more complex illustration of sacred geometry.

In the progression of the torus, each circle within the circle can be interpreted as a cycle within the Mayan calendar. Just as the Mayan calendar has nine parts, so does the torus. As each of the different cycles is added within the interior of the main circle, their interactions, patterns, and combinations become more complex in motion until, ultimately, perfect form is attained. As the formation progresses, the internal harmonics change; these harmonics include both true frequencies and implied tones, just like the harmonic octave. At times, the interior of the circle becomes harmonically resonant, and at other times, a sense of imbalance, or lack of harmonic resonance, occurs in the interior. At the moment perfect form occurs—at the culmination, the Grand Year, 2012—perfect resonance happens.

The Flower of Life and the Tree of Life

In the sixth stage of the interweaving of energies that builds the torus, we see that a Flower of Life is formed.

The Flower of Life has six petals. In the Mayan calendar, there are six major cycles in the Grand Year. Further, the combined upright and inverted pyramids in the form of the tetrahedron fit perfectly within the

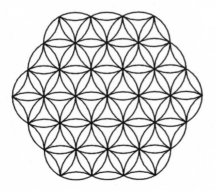

The Flower of Life in the Great Cycles.

The star tetrahedron fits perfectly in each section of the Flower of Life. These sections are sometimes known as the seeds of life.

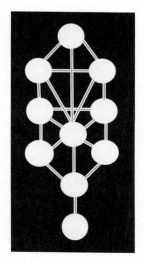

The Cabala's Tree of Life matches the
Mayan's Sacred Tree (Graphic by author).

The Sacred Tree, or Tree of Life, fites within the
Flower of Life.

Flower of Life. This exact fit can be interpreted as symbolizing how, upon
the completion of each of the cycles in the Mayan calendar, there will be
perfect balance and a heightening of harmonic frequencies that leads to
a period of greater consciousness awareness.

As the six cycles progress, full harmonic resonance occurs, and we
end up with what the Mayans called the Sacred Tree. In the Cabala, this
tree is called the Tree of Life. The Sacred Tree has nine stations plus its
point of beginning, or its base, just as the Mayan calendar has nine parts
when we add the six major cycles and the three subcycles of the Long
Count. Geometrically, the Sacred Tree nests perfectly within the Flower
of Life. This is no coincidence!

The totality of all the cycles culminates at the moment we reach the
Grand Year—in this case, 2012. Each petal of the Flower of Life represents a basic cycle in the Mayan calendar. Each cycle is a progression of
consciousness in time. Each cycle combined with the progressive others takes us further and further around the progression, first through
periods of enlightenment, then into long stages of darkness, and then
back toward and ultimately into the light as we return full circle to our
center.

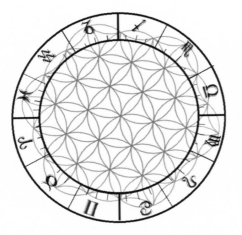

Astrology wheel overlaying the Flower of Life (graphic by author).

Notice that all of the cycles are interlinked within the Flower of Life, and the Sacred Tree (Tree of Life) links everything together. This geometric set is representative of the infinite and repetitive structure of the cycles of creation, of consciousness, and even of reality. When one studies the Cabala and its Tree of Life, one almost immediately realizes that the concepts contained within it have multiple meanings, often of great depth.

With the culmination of the Mayan calendar in December of 2012, we have a perfect completion and joining of the Mayan calendar, the Flower of Life, the Cabala, and the star tetrahedron. Perfection on every level. We also have the completion of the astrology wheel, which also lays over the Flower of Life perfectly with each outside circle, coinciding with one sign all the way around the wheel.

Carried just a little further, in the geometry of the moment that the Mayan calendar culminates its cycle, a few more things happen. Remember how the Sacred Tree or Tree of Life locks in the aspects of the Flower of Life? And how the star tetrahedron overlays the Flower of Life so beautifully? Well, the star tetrahedron (the true trinity) also incorporates the Tree of Life and within it the cross, the sign of Christianity. In Muslim symbol-

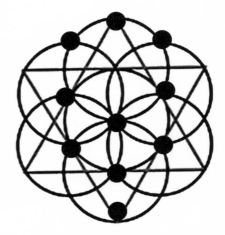

The Cabala's Tree of Life within the star tetrahedron and the Flower of Life (graphic by author)

ogy we find the star tetrahedron with the god energy in the center from the perspective of the bases. The star tetrahedron is also associated with Judaism. In other words, at the moment of alignment, the symbolism of most all of the major religions of our world also come together. This symbol has been used in churches all over the globe and by the Knights Templar and Masons in their buildings, such as cathedrals and churches.

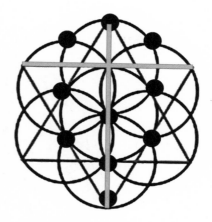

The Flower of Life, the Cabala's Tree of Life, and the Christian cross join as the Mayan calendar culminates. (graphic by author).

As we begin each cycle, we move into higher vibrations of energy, higher harmonic frequencies, and, therefore, opportunities for the expansion of our consciousness. As the Flower of Life comes together geometrically, in that process there are periods of harmonic imbalance. It is during those times that we fall into dark ages, periods of struggle and negativity, times of power and destruction. As the cycles progress, greater and greater balance occurs, and we begin to crawl out of the darkness and back to the light, to higher consciousness, and a feeling of greater connection with our source.

The Pivotal Center of the Torus

When we come to the end of the fifth Great Cycle, we will have reached a pivotal moment in our existence and the existence of reality as we know it. As noted earlier, the moment of our perfect alignment at the galactic center is represented by the torus. The center, or divine core, that we saw in the circle (as the most basic geometric form) and in the torus tube is not only the anchor point, but also a balance point. *It is the center of both consumption and creation.*

The center point of the torus represents the universe with a black hole at the center; the combination of man and God, like we saw in the

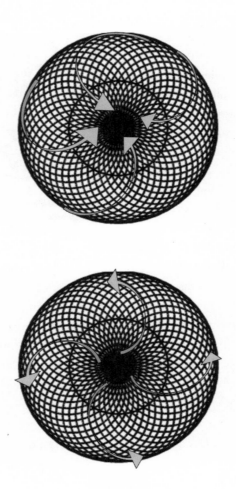

Polarities and energy flow changes of the torus. The top figure shows positive polarity as energy cascades over the torus walls and into the center. The bottom figure shows negative polarity where energy flows on the outside of the torus walls into a burst of creation. (Graphic by author)

circle; the process of creation as it uses and creates energy; and the transition of consciousness from enlightenment to darkness and back again.
In other words, in the torus, we see day 0.0.0.0.0 to day 13.0.0.0.0 of
the Mayan calendar. As the harmonics within the calendar change, the
numbers in the decimal places also change until the Grand Year, or in
our case, 2012, is reached.

The energies within the torus do not stay in one place. They move
around the curved sides of the torus and through the center. The center
is a transitional point for the energies. It is in this center that energy is
both used and created in a natural flow. Time in the Mayan calendar
does the same thing.

Depending upon internal and external influences, such as the harmonic frequencies, the polarities within the torus tube can also change.
When the flow of energy is in a positive polarity, the energies, or cycles of
the calendar, all move toward the center of the circle, round and round
down through the circle, like water down a drain. Then the energies flow
back up over the curved edges toward the source point in the center,
where they fall through the opening like a cascading waterfall.

In a reverse or negative polarity, the energy moves in just the opposite
way. The moment that the polarities change is a beginning point, a point
of creation. As the polarity shifts, there is a miniscule pause or moment
of stillness within the torus, and then the energy begins to move again.
The polarity reverses, and the energy starts flowing in the opposite direction. The energy now moves from the source point outward, like a foun-
tain, across the *top* of the circle, cascading around the sides of the torus
and back toward the center underneath. In this polarity, energy shoots
out of the center at the top of the circle as a point of release, which is also
a beginning, or creation moment.

Whether being of positive or negative polarity, the energy that moves
through the torus constantly feeds the source point in the center, and
new light energy and momentum of energy flow is created.

Our galaxy has a center, too. As our solar system moves in all of its
intricate patterns, (with all its aspects tracked by the Mayan calendar), it
ultimately reaches the center of its beginning, the galactic center. At the

galactic center, there is great light that some call the photon belt. That light or photon belt is an expansion of energy that is our galactic balance point. In other words, the movement of our solar system and other bodies within our galaxy are of a similar construct and act in the exact same way as the inner workings of the torus tube.

This magnificent geometric formation also occurs when we reach fully enlightened consciousness. In the moments that we access gamma consciousness, our consciousness is participating, without resistance, in the true format of creation. In those moments, we are truly going with the flow, completely aware of everything and nothing.

Just like when we reach gamma consciousness, as time passes within each set of cycles of the Mayan calendar, the sections of the calendar are laced together, forming the same energy and harmonic frequencies that we saw in the combined pyramids of the true trinity—the combination of us, creation, and creation and us! We can geometrically link this process with the pyramid, the star tetrahedron, the Flower of Life, and the torus.

Remember the spheres within the pyramids? As the upright and inverted pyramids are combined, the two spheres press against each other and begin to wobble out of balance. From there, they momentarily flatten and then spontaneously form a singular torus tube, which ultimately balances into a singular sphere! More simply put, the torus is at the center of creation, where time and consciousness are universally connected!

In response to the cycles of energy movement, which are tracked by the calendars provided to us by the Mayans, our consciousness goes through periods of darkness and enlightenment. From the beginning of the sixth petal of the Flower of Life—or last consecutive Great Cycle, as the Mayans called it—until the moment of culmination of the Grand Year, our consciousness unfolds like the petals of a lotus until we reach a point of pure awareness—or, conversely, by resistance to our natural evolution, a period of total destruction. (More about the potential destruction later.)

When we observe the basic geometric illustration of creation (see page 148), we can imagine that as our solar system moves within the universal torus, there comes a moment in time when we are fed back to the beginning of this cyclic pattern, right to the very center, our original beginning point. This point is filled with light—the light of creation. It is this light that is considered by many to be the photon belt. The amplified light in the photon belt near the center of our origin acts as a stimulus to consciousness. Remember, we are created of the same light!

During this period of movement, which is actually several years *before* and *after* the actual moment of alignment, we have a window for the complete reharmonization of consciousness—a resetting, if you will, of consciousness and energy in creation as we know it. During the time that our solar system moves into, centers, and then moves out of our galactic center, we experience stimulation by the light of our beginning, just like in the model of consciousness that we talked about in Chapter Three.

At the very instance that our solar system reaches its beginning point, the center of our galaxy, there will be a nearly immeasurable pause and a slight backward spin of the earth, just as when the torus changes polarities. This is a cosmic pause, a reset of cosmic proportions, that basically disconnects all forms of learned beings from pure existence in a way that is much like a momentary blanking out of our consciousness circuits. At that point, those of us who are very sensitive to energy may feel a small blip in our awareness or a stutter in our thought patterns. (Some of us may feel nothing at all.) When this pause happens, we literally begin a new cycle of consciousness that will last nearly 26,000 years. This cycle will ebb and flow just as all other cycles before it, bringing times of enlightenment and periods of darkness in cycles similar to the ones the Mayan people laid out in their calendar system.

We Have a Choice

At the moment of the slight wobble, there is an opportunity, energetically and harmonically, for the poles of the torus of reality to shift from a positive to a negative polarity. If that were to happen, our planet would almost definitely follow suit, and our magnetic north and south poles would change from north to south and from south to north. This kind of an event would be catastrophic, causing a great ice age in areas where there are now tropical forests, severe volcanic eruptions, immense seismic activity, severe weather, failure of our electrical systems, and even some changes to our atmosphere as the ions change polarity. The setup occurs as we approach our galactic center.

But this catastrophic polarity shift doesn't have to happen!

The beauty of all of the interrelations described in preceding pages is that they show us that our Consciousness works from within the construct of creation. In other words, we are the consciousness within the living One. Because of this, we have the power to create whatever reality we desire during the time preceding the alignment. During this time, as the reharmonization occurs, our intentions, the messages that we send out to creation, will become reality. We are truly in a shift of ages, a crux point, a pivotal moment in the evolution of consciousness, reality, and the human race.

As fundamental aspects of the construct of reality, each of us is uniquely harmonized. As integral parts of creation, we have the power to create whatever outcome we desire simply by intending it. Wow! Now *that* is power!

We can choose to follow the herd mentality, fearing our demise, and ride into the fire with our eyes closed, or we can become proactive, projecting positive outcome into the process of creation.

As noted in Chapter Six, the shift toward 2012 actually began on March 3, 2003. That date, when represented numerically, is a triple trinity of three 3s (3/3/03):

3 (March, the third month of the year)

3 (the third day of the month)

3 ('03)

Added together, these three 3s add up to 9, which numerologically signifies culmination, or an end. The triple harmony once again is indicative of the true trinity: us, creation, and us and creation. (Where have we heard that before?)

(Some readers may say, "Wait a minute! This is really a 3-3-5 harmonization if you use 2003 instead of '03." In that case, we get a number

11, which is a key number in numerology and singularly represents the energy of the source.)

As the shift commenced on March 3, 2003, we eased out of old harmonics and into the beginning of the reharmonization that precedes the culmination of the Grand Year. At that time, we began to shift out of old paradigms and into more open, progressive perspectives.

There is no escape. We are intrinsically interwoven into the fabric of creation. It affects us, and we affect it as we live in an infinite choreography of events, reality, and creation. What will we do with this newfound realization? Will we choose to live it, being the powerful creators that we truly are? Or will we choose to remain oblivious to things unseen, unfelt, but very, very real? It is truly up to each of us.

Additional Contributing Factors

There are additional factors that can affect our 2012 experience. One of the major players is our sun. The sun has cycles in which it becomes more active, throwing solar flares out from its surface. These flares are what we call coronal mass ejections (CMEs), or massive emissions of electromagnetic energy. As the flares rise violently from the sun's molten surface, they shoot outward, away from the sun. CMEs are shaped kind of like a slice of pie, wide at the front and narrow on the back end.

As the ejection of this seemingly unstoppable energy occurs, the wide front of the emission barrels toward our planet and collides with our atmosphere with great force. When the collision takes place, our atmosphere is pushed toward the earth and compacted. At the moment of greatest compression, the electromagnetic force of the CME springs back, in the same way that we rise in the air after jumping down on a trampoline.

CMEs affect how we feel, our moods, our bodies—everything. Some people can actually feel the solar flares as they happen; other people respond as our atmosphere is compressed, but don't know why they feel like they do. These reactions happen because the solar flare's compression of our atmosphere affects our very particulates, condensing our energies momentarily. In those moments, we are being energetically squished.

During periods of heavy solar flares, satellites are affected, as are electrical grids. Further, radio and TV signals are disrupted momentarily, and even aeronautic navigation systems are adversely affected. In fact, anything that uses electricity or fine electromagnetic energy can be scrambled by a CME.

If we happen to be in a period of high solar-flare activity as we click with our galactic center, CMEs can also affect the internal resonance of the toroid center of the earth. Because the interior of the earth is an electromagnetic field, it could respond to the effects of a huge CME in conjunction with the influences of our Grand Day alignment. In that case, we could have a full or partial shift of our magnetic poles.

What we need to remember is that our sun and our earth, like us, are within the toroid structure of creation on all levels and are, therefore, affected by consciousness, just like everything else.

Interdimensional events also affect us whether we realize it or not. When the star-gate systems and wormholes open, they generally create first an imbalance of energy and harmonics and then an internal balance within creation. They act as vacuums of energy, dispersing building energies much more quickly, so that those energies don't build up to a point of huge release. The transition of energy becomes much gentler in its balance.

Because our consciousness has a huge effect on reality, by virtue of our willingness and intentions, we have the capability to create a smooth transition in and out of the 2012 alignment. More and more people are awakening to the fact that we have choices to make and the possibility that realities beyond our third dimension really do exist. This awakening has appeared limited and has the nature of a grassroots movement, but it is truly part of a much bigger picture: the evolution of humanity back toward the light of our creation.

If you have any doubt at all that there are enough of us to create these kinds of changes, think again. *There are millions and millions of people on the planet who are all working in their own ways to create a positive shift in 2012.*

The most efficient way to create a positive shift is by all of us coming together with a singular intention: to create a positive outcome. The details don't really matter, because each of us has a frame of reference that is ours alone. Instead of details based upon each of our singular perceptions, we must focus on positive outcomes. All we need to project is how we will feel when we are using all of our senses as we experience whatever reality we intend to create during and beyond 2012. The best way to do this projection is for all of us, at a designated moment, to open our hearts and imagine *how we will feel* when we have experienced the *positive outcome* and the fullness of everything the shift has to offer us. If we do this with an open heart and project *no details*, only our feelings, that reality will create powerfully and quickly. The language of the heart is universal. It moves quickly and unerringly throughout creation, communicating in the highest of frequencies and the purest of form.

As 2012 looms, I will be creating an event based upon the setup of the harmonics in which we can all get together to project this feeling. When we gather, each additional one of us magnifies the outcome exponentially as our energies travel within creation. This is a measurable phenomenon with immeasurable possibilities. How will we imagine our future? What will we create together as an outcome? I say, choose positive polarity and light.

Signs the Shift Is Affecting Us

We now know all of the intricacies of the current shift of ages, of energy, of creation, and of our world within creation. But how do times like these affect us as individuals?

Sadly, we are often so busy living our lives within the illusions that we have created for ourselves that we are completely unaware of our more subtle experiences. As the energies within creation change, we change too. Our very particulates become reharmonized, and we are changed energetically. In fact, we are affected mentally, physically, spiritually, and emotionally by changes in our subtle energy fields. These subtle fields are very finely tuned harmonically, and when there are changes in them, we feel those changes. We just aren't always aware of the experience. Sometimes our awareness of the energy changes is intense and powerfully disturbing. At other times, when the changes are much more subtle, they sneak past us as we blur through our fast-paced lives.

Here are just some of the ways we experience the shift:

Labile moods: Subtle or powerful mood swings. One moment we are on top of the world, and the next we have unexplainable sadness or anger. We may experience periods of great sadness with no obvious cause or, conversely, periods of elation, also for no apparent reason. This symptom may also include emotional outbursts that are intense, but generally short-lived. These outbursts occur because old emotions that we have hidden from ourselves, in an attempt to deny them, are being released as we reharmonize.

Fluctuating physical energy levels: We change from fully energized to absolutely exhausted, and vice versa, at the drop of a hat.

Fluctuating subtle energy levels: Feeling at times as if we have been plugged into an electrical socket, as if we might explode from the energy buildup inside of us. At other times, feeling completely ungrounded and nearly disassociated from our current reality.

Physical pain: May be in the form of mild, but inexplicable background headaches, joint pain, muscle pain, or even nerve pain at times when we become overcharged with the changing harmonics.

Greater sensitivity: Feeling with one's entire being, not just with the five senses. One might notice changes in energy, stronger feelings around other people and places, more intuitive impressions.

Intense dreaming: Busy dreamtimes; dreams with a great deal of symbolism, deeper meaning, or intensity, or dreams that don't seem to make sense at all.

Brain fog: The inability to maintain focus or to feel that things make sense. Sometimes this fog means having trouble finding the words we want to say, and other times it means having words become tangled up when we try to express ourselves.

Changes in diet: No longer liking foods that used to be your favorites. Craving foods we never used to like or care about, or that are very different from our usual preferences.

Digestive sensitivity: Tendencies toward constipation or diarrhea, or having unpredictable reactions to foods.

Lack of concentration or decisiveness: When the energies within us are temporarily disharmonic or not acclimated to the current changes, we experience a lack of ability to focus. Often during these same disharmonics, we have a hard time making decisions, even when we are usually very decisive.

Memory issues: When the energy is at more intense stages during the shift, our short-term memory is affected. We have trouble remembering earlier today, yesterday, or last week. At extreme times, even our long-term memory suffers for a short time.

Unusual awareness: We begin to awaken to realities other than the one with which we are familiar. We might spontaneously become intuitive, knowing things before they happen or what others are thinking. Further, we might begin to have glimpses of other realities; these glimpses may appear as blips out of the sides of our eyes, as people, as animals, or perhaps even as things unexplained.

Full-blown awakening: Consciousness expands spontaneously, and other realities are experienced in varying ways. We might begin to see or even talk with other kinds of beings, such as angels, guides from other realms, or even those who have died and are now on "the other side." These experiences can be very disconcerting and a real challenge to one's sense of reality. If such experiences happen, remember that we are always in charge of our experience and have the option to change it at any time.

Relationship issues: Remember, just as we are affected during the shifting energies, so is everyone else. We all react differently. When we enter into relationships, we harmonize with the other person or people. As the changes of the shift reharmonize us, we may no longer be in harmony within our relationships. Our relationships may become challenging, or they may no longer fit us. Remember that, if this is the case, we will develop other relationships that are completely in harmony with us.

Lack of tolerance for untruths: As our particulates change harmonization within creation and ourselves, the harmonics become so fine that there is no room for untruth. In fact, developing a drive to seek truth in everything is not unusual.

The need for isolation: This is due to heightened sensitivity and, as a result, the need for balance. Isolation can be very healing at times, but too much can be detrimental.

Interruption of sleep patterns: Sleeping intermittently, having difficulty falling asleep on high-energy days, or feeling the need to sleep much longer than usual.

Fear: The unknown can be daunting, and as we come closer and closer to 2012, there will be a lot of media hype, a lot of books written, and movies and TV programs on the subject. The important thing to remember is our personal truth. Knowing how creation works and that we are integral parts of its reality gives us the freedom to understand that reality is what we create, not what we fear it might be.

Changes in global relations: These changes are less personal, but are still definite signs of shifting. These changes come in two forms. The first is conflict for political or religious gain, or power struggles between countries, factions, races, or tribes, and the escalated terroristic, murderous, warring treatment of one branch of humanity by another. The second form of changes is positive, such as changes in political climates and in the priorities of world leaders. For example, we are beginning to glimpse the political awareness of a need for a global network that works for the good of *all* the people of our planet—a one-world scenario in which our resources are shared, people are educated, and funding is provided to improve their conditions (and they don't have to fear that improvements will be taken from them). That one-world perspective will happen—and it must happen, if we are to survive.

Of course, if any of the physical or mental symptoms listed continue for a prolonged amount of time, they could be caused by something other than the shifting energies. If that is the case, seek assistance from someone who is qualified. For the most part, the symptoms above will come and go, being intense, but short-lived.

The shift that we are experiencing can affect each individual any combination of the ways above, or even in other, more subtle ways. The intensity of these symptoms will escalate as the energies prepare for the 2012 alignment. We may see new or additional symptoms as well.

The important thing to remember is to be aware of what your experience is. Awareness brings ease in a lot of cases. Often, we struggle against the unknown, blaming ourselves for outside influences that had nothing to do with us. When we become aware, the fear factor disintegrates, and our comfort zone is magnified greatly.

Now more than ever it is important to be fully aware of what we are going through, both internally and externally. Self-awareness is tantamount to comfort in the coming times. Our goal should be to have our internal experiences match our external ones. Then, and only then, are we fully balanced and able to intentionally and purely participate in creating a positive outcome for the shift. If we are not balanced inside or out, we are indirectly and subconsciously contributing to a powerfully negative outcome.

It doesn't take the entire world population to make positive change—only a group of balanced human beings, all sending the same intention into the creative process, and fueling that intention with passion for that change. The more of us who have expanded awareness, the more others will also experience it. As more and more of us awaken to greater reality, what we feel and know becomes part of the mass consciousness. We can see this dynamic right now in the expanded vocabulary of consciousness being used in the media, in movies, and in society in general. Hollywood often picks up on trends in the mass consciousness long before the public at large does.

We have developed a momentum toward a moment of critical mass, when the awareness of our perfection and all that it contains snaps back into us like a cosmic two-by-four hitting us across our heads. As each one of us evolves consciously, so does everything else. As the energy of our mass consciousness harmonizes into perfect resonance, we will become spontaneously attuned to greater awareness.

Flowing With the Shift: Eight Keys

Practically applying what we now know is really very easy. It is about being who we are. Let go of the drama and trauma that is caused by the fear of everyday life. Live fully. Breathe, relax, and, to paraphrase the Hopi, don't try to hang onto the sides of the river, for there you will surely drown. Let go of the weeds and go with the flow, and you will be effortlessly carried along the way.

Unobstructed by the past and future and, at the same time, fueled by them in every now, our consciousness has the potential to blow wide open in the coming years. We have learned together just how easy it is to create reality. We have learned that we are infinite beings within the construct of creation and that in our infinite being we can change our reality just by choosing differently than we have in the past. In fact, we can change our reality just by choosing at all.

Generally speaking, human beings don't change their ways unless some stimulus forces that change. Change is scary for us because it takes us outside of our comfortable norm. We tend to fight change, kicking and screaming the entire way, immersing ourselves in the chaos that has been created exclusively by us and our resistance. Truly, though, if we choose to accept and not resist change, the result of chaos is magnificence.

Here are eight keys to help you create universal change from the inside out. These few powerful steps can change not only your life, but also the lives of those around you. Don't worry about the intangible. Just because you can't see it, feel it, smell it, hear it, or taste it doesn't mean it isn't real.

The following eight keys for surviving the shift are great tools for life. They are based upon the same progressive harmonics that are found in sacred geometry as the upright and inverted pyramids are combined to form a star tetrahedron, an eight-pointed star. The energy of each key is a harmonic point of the star.

These eight truths are eternal. One without the other isn't a full set, just as we alone are not. Yet each key is part of the whole, just as you are part of all that is and has ever been.

1. **Acknowledge your perfection.** Perfection begets perfection. Imagining yourself as anything less than perfect is purely a learned perception. Look beyond what you have been conditioned to believe, and embrace your infinite perfect self.

2. **Accept the journey for which you have come.** Live your life fully; don't sit around and wait for life to come to you! In order to reap the rewards of your intentions, you must pray *and* move your feet!

3. **Maintain personal integrity.** Who we are in ourselves has everything to do with our outward experience. Be true to yourself, no matter what. Tell yourself the truth and don't doubt yourself for a minute. Once you have learned to be honest within, being honest with the rest of the world is easy, because you no longer have anything to hide.

4. **Be who you are, not how you think others would see you.** You are created of light, of grace, and of only that which is of truth. You are a living image of creation. You do not need to improve yourself, and there is nothing to heal. You have only to be who you have always been. Get to know yourself. You will love who you find.

5. **Accept your power.** You are great and mighty. True power comes not from ego, but from the collective One of your spirit, your very being. True power is gentle power. You are of the light, and in its seemingly nebulous construct is the essence from which all things are made. To fear inner power suggests that you are less than all other things. In Truth, power is of grace, and not

abusiveness or aggressiveness. Embrace the power of your spirit, of living intentionally as the co-creator of everything that you seek.

6.   **Acknowledge your value.** This is different than accepting perfection. Your value is how you fit within your *interior* world, as well as the exterior world in which you exist. You are created of that which is all things, and all things are you. Therefore, there can be no one and nothing lesser or greater than you. When your internal and external worlds feel the same, you have found true balance. This balance has everything to do with your recognition of value, for when you are out of balance you are out of truth and cannot find your value.

7.   **Take your value, your perfection, your power, and your grace into your world.** Change comes only from practicing change. What this means is that to effect change, you must embody it. Walk your talk; do not hide what you know or who you are. Historically, what is hidden is later viewed as heresy in relation to the accepted norm, or worse, forgotten completely. To change this dynamic, create a new accepted norm with ease and grace by virtue of walking within the very light from which you are created.

8.   **Love yourself, and touch everyone you encounter with love.** True love is a state of being, which you find when you have accepted yourself as a perfect and integral part of the One. What will you accept from others, and what will you leave behind? See everyone as a loving mirror of yourself, that their pain resides somewhere within you, and that their joy is in your heart as well. This is why random acts of kindness make such a difference. Remember the saying, "There, but for the grace of God, go I"? It is so. It has always been so.

And, of course, remember to breathe. Your breath does more than just oxygenate your body. Your breath clears and nurtures you energetically. Each breath is a cleansing, and as you are cleansed, your energy system moves more easily and communicates with greater clarity within the universal consciousness, communicating your experience as well as what your experience can be. When you do not breathe because you are tense, your entire energy system compacts and becomes more and more sluggish. As a result, your creative process becomes sluggish or even stalled. Breathe!

As you live these eight keys, imagine what the world will be like post-2012. How will it change for the better? How will you feel when you have arrived in that moment of time? Believe these feelings to be so, and you will have just created that new reality. There will be a moment in time when you and your new reality meet, and it will be perfection!

Meditation 7

Inner Harmony

As you encounter the symbol in the illustration to the left, imagine that you are a vessel filled with water. Imagine that water surrounds your vessel as well. Is the pressure, the water level, that you feel on the inside equal to the pressure of the water on your exterior? If not, knowing that water seeks its own level, ask that the waters within and around you flow to or from you toward balance, until there is no difference in what you feel inside and out, and the water is even in and around you. Feel the ease of this new equilibrium. What you feel is harmonic balance, the attunement of your inner world with the world around you and, therefore, with all of creation.

Chapter Eight

Beyond 2012:
What Does Our Future Hold?

Is There Life After 2012?

The year 2012 is surrounded by speculation, excitement, and even fear. Throughout this book, we have looked deeply and fully at not only the reasons for the end of the Mayan calendar, but also the possibilities of beginning a new cycle. Whether we realize it or not, we are already attuning to future events. Every particulate in our bodies has risen to the occasion. Like lizards basking in the sun, we are sleepily absorbing light in the form of changing energies. In our laziness, something is happening. Our dreams are changing. The dream of our reality is changing. Our consciousness is expanding. Inside of us, something is stirring. We are beginning to feel as if something huge is about to happen.

It is.

But it isn't the end of the world.

It is humanity coming to a place of resonance within creation. It is a snapping together, if you will, of pieces of a great puzzle to form a magnificent picture of reality. Our Grand Day is coming, and after the party is over, a new day will come. As we move out of the galactic center on a new 26,000-year adventure, our awareness will continue to rise for centuries. The numbers of possibilities for a greater tomorrow are beyond our scope of imagining.

At the same time that we come into this grand resonance, other events will be shaping up. The harmonics of our new journey are going to have infinite effect on not only us, but also on our planet and all of creation. Remember, everything affects everything. We are masters within an infinite choreography that responds in every moment to all that occurs.

A partial shift of the earth's poles may occur, but it will not be disastrous. If a partial shift happens, it will cause some change to climate and weather patterns, but that is nothing new. We, as a race, have migrated naturally across our lands as long as we have existed.

Within humanity, we will begin to witness trends toward greater humanitarianism and a more unified world. This will take some time, but the signs are already visible.

Interdimensionally, there is a refinement of harmonics happening that will bring the second level of gamma consciousness, communion consciousness, more to the surface of our awareness. We will begin to spontaneously experience what was taught in the mystery schools in darker times.

But that is only the beginning.

Harmonic Alignment of the Pyramids in 2018

You may remember from Chapter Two that all of the pyramids are individually harmonized, each with a unique set of frequencies, just like each of us. Their individual harmonics are due to their locations having different resonance in and upon the earth, their relations to celestial bodies, the angulations at which they are built, and even their methods and materials of construction. But there is more.

From 2012 to 2015, as the earth pulls away from the galactic center and new and different electromagnetic forces begin to have an influence, the energies upon our planet will reharmonize as well. The ley lines of the earth will change frequencies, moving toward a completely new harmonic resonance within creation. As that occurs, we will respond dramatically. We will literally feel lighter in our existence and not as heavily grounded, as gravitational forces will also vary somewhat while the new resonance amplifies.

As the ley lines upon the earth take on a new harmonic resonance, there will be a rising of energies in very fine frequencies. If we could see this rise, it would look a lot like someone started to turn up a dimmer switch to create a brighter light. In this case, the light will rise from the earth.

As the frequencies of light become brighter upon the earth, on March 27, 2018 at 5:56 p.m. central time, there will be a monumental event. This event marks the coming of the 11:11 harmonics that so many of us have been seeing on our clocks, our computers, on signs all around us for several years. The 11:11 has been a symbol of warning for us for years. The 11:11 shows us the perfect balance of the above and the below, the inside and the exterior, the past and the present, and more. As above, so below: in the heavens and on the earth, an event of great significance will occur.

In that moment, all of the pyramid sites on the planet will slide into a harmonic alignment, which will create a unified resonance among all pyramids.

This resonance will send a message of galactic proportions out through our solar system, across our galaxy and even into parallel realities. From great distances, it will appear as if a star has been born, and that star is planet earth. This harmonic resonance among the pyramids will act as a portal for incoming energies, which will crack the nut of our mentality and create a further opening to awakening far beyond the energies of 2012. This alignment will also act as a beacon for those of other-than-terrestrial residence to come to earth once again.

The harmonic alignment and resonance of the pyramids will take place in three stages over about nine months. At the pinnacle of the harmonic alignment, as the energies of the pyramid harmonization align universally, there will be a spontaneous alignment and opening of yet another series of star gates. This star-gate system is from the before times, before we have a record of history. It lies like a blanket across universes, reaching far into creation and opening doors of awareness and travel that were used by three of the root races who contributed to the evolution of humanity as they visited our planet.

The most amazing thing about this particular star-gate system is that it is shaped like the Tree of Life, which is also known as the Cabala. (See Chapter Seven.) The Tree of Life, or Cabala, is hidden in the geometry of the Flower of Life. It is a set of frequencies that are very close to the harmonics of our source and relate intricately with every aspect of who and what we are. The Cabala is one of the great ancient mysteries that people study diligently in order to find the deeper meaning of life. Its meanings are holographic, multileveled. The more one understands about its meanings, the more questions there are to be asked.

It is this Sacred Tree that the Mayan calendar referred to.

There is no escaping the ancient references to these times. We are intricately laced—past, present, and future—into the fabric of reality. The time for the unfolding of our being is now.

The Last Chapter?

Our ancient predecessors did not survive the changes that took place in a past that is beyond our memories. We really don't know why, so we are left to speculate. While it is true that history often repeats itself, it is also true that we have the intelligence to learn from what we do know and to effect whatever changes are necessary toward altering the outcome of any event or series of events.

Previous civilizations, whether in times of expanded consciousness or periods of darkness, faltered and fizzled because they became overconfident of their perceptions of power and their technologies. Some of them, like the Atlanteans, learned to live in harmony with the planet and beyond, until egos created a disastrous series of events from which there was no escape. Others, like the Sumerians, the Mayans, and the ancient Egyptians, knew how to track the planetary movements, the stars, and their importance to life on earth. But events like asteroid collisions with the earth, global flooding, and more got the best of them in the end. Their bravado closed the door to their greater awareness to the point that not only were they not listening anymore to their greater intuitive nature, but they also forgot how to hear entirely.

We have a different set of ears. We have the benefit of the energies of the Grand Day, a culmination of the Great Cycles, all coming together in our lifetime to foster within us a new beginning.

Technology is a double-edged sword. It can make things convenient, measurable, fast, communicative, and even destructive. The key is to know that our technologies are only creations that we make to mirror what we are capable of from within our infinite consciousness.

The Internet, for example, is a mirror of our infinite consciousness. We have created something that we can experience outside of ourselves and that brings us seemingly unlimited information. Our consciousness can do that without all of the machinery, if we can free our perceptions enough to let go of the need to know and open ourselves to the vastness of what is available to us from creation.

We often have the perception that technology ensures our safety and our survival. But it can also be our downfall, because with it we gain a false confidence and stop doing our part to move toward positive outcomes. Humanity overall has become less than diligent about its future. We have become numb to the subtleties of our world that would, if noticed, tell us everything that we need to know. Some call the subtleties guidance. The truth is that the subtleties are more than that. They are our greater, more expanded selves bringing us messages time and again to get us on track with where we really want to be. Yet instead of listening to or following our inner guidance, we try to force things to happen.

When we act against the natural flow, we get unnatural results.

Unlike our ancient predecessors, we have the ability to look in our rearview mirrors to see how and perhaps even why those who came before us didn't survive. We have the possibility of recognizing where humanity has failed previously, and we have the intelligence to change our direction. But are we doing that?

Some of us are.

It is interesting how we split ourselves into factions or groups by which we are identified. Subconsciously, we need to belong, because on some level we truly do know that we are part of a great whole. Now we just need to bring that perception to the forefront of our awareness and work together toward a common goal, a positive outcome, a symbiosis of us as a collective with all of creation. This isn't a fantasy or some "woo-woo" concept. It is a very real possibility, and it isn't too late.

If we take the information in this book and live it with clear intentions, we can create whatever world we want. We can build a momentum of consciousness like none that has ever happened in the history of humanity.

If we could just take a moment and consider how tiny we are in relation to all of creation, we might gain a more humble perspective. Our egos have soared, fueled by the lies we tell ourselves to convince us that we are, individually, the most important creatures in creation. We must look past the illusion of our egos and into what is real.

The reality is that we are whole and perfect sons and daughters of creation. We are living expressions of the One. While each of us is a unique and powerful expression of creation, together we are a massive consciousness borne of the light and capable of instigating reality and guiding events, and, on the flip side, instigating our destruction. Will we harmonize together? If so, how will we? Only time will tell.

We must know that we are all after the same thing. We just haven't gotten our acts together for that common purpose. As successful as we are in our own rights, imagine what we could do if we came together with common goals, coalescing our consciousnesses to work in sync toward a greater reality. Imagine how it could be if we stopped looking at each other's differences and started looking instead at the possibilities those differences have to contribute. The ancients left us a road map for doing so.

Together, we are the whole picture. Individually, we are just drops of ink on a page that is too close to the fire. In order to move beyond the fire, we must become it. Be the flames. Be the heat. Be the smoke that permeates everything in creation. Most of all, we must be the light that is a beacon to a greater tomorrow.

Because we can.

We know.

We are.

That.

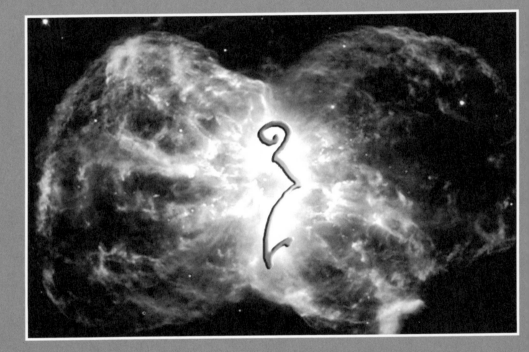

Meditation 8

Courage Amid Change

Look deep within yourself. Can you find the innocence you felt as a child? That sense of wonderment when you encountered something new and exciting? As a child, you didn't hesitate to explore whatever piqued your curiosity. Instead, you leapt into discovering it. Imagine how you can bring that childlike curiosity into this now, bringing excitement for the changes to come and your imaginings about what magic those changes will bring to you.

Bibliography

Online Sources

2012 Nostradamus. Web site. Available at *www.2012nostradamus.com.* All about the Nostradamus prophesies, especially relative to 2012.

All About 2012. Web site. Available at *www.greatdreams.com/2012.htm.* Great site about ancient technologies, 2012, and sacred geometry.

Burlington UFO and Paranormal Research and Education Center. "Dogons Could Hold the Answer to the Mysteries of Our Past." Web site. Available at *www.burlingtonnews.net/dogons.html.* Site with audio interviews, articles, and more multimedia related to Dogons.

Coppins, Phillip. "Let There Be Light!" Web site. Available at *www.philipcoppens.com/denderah.html.* Images of ancient carvings of light bulbs at Dendera in Egypt.

Crop Circle Connector. Web site. Available at *www.cropcircleconnector.com.* The best and most up-to-date crop circle site I have found.

December 21, 2012. Web site. Available at *www.december212012.com.* Numerous articles about 2012.

Downs, Dennielle, and Ava Meyerhoff. "Battery, Baghdad, 250 BCE." Smith College History of Science: Museum of Ancient Inventions. Edited by Marjorie Senechal. Available at *www.smith.edu.* More about the Baghdad battery.

The Galactic Alignment. Web site. Available at *http://pperov.angelfire.com/galactic.html.* In-depth information about the galactic alignment.

The Golden Age Project. Web site. Available at *www.goldenageproject.org.uk.* Documents and papers pertaining to changing our perspective about history.

Gowan, John A. *General Systems, Gravity, and the Unified Field Theory.* Web site. Available at *www.johnagowan.org.* Essays on fractals, cosmology, theory of everything, time, entropy, weak and strong forces, science and religion, life, the human condition.

"HTHistory Chapter 2 Lesson Plans." *India History Resources.* Second of six lesson plans prepared by *Hinduism Today* to assist educators teaching Hindu history. Available at *www.scribd.com.* Contains excellent information about ancient India's flying machines.

Jefferys, John. "Brain Waves ("40 Hz") Research." University of Birmingham Neurophysiology Department, University of Birmingham Web site, *http://www.web-us.com/40HZ/default.htm.* October 2003.

NOVA: *Magnetic Storm.* Companion Web site for the NOVA episode "Magnetic Storm," which aired November 18, 2003, on PBS. Available at *www.pbs.org.* Offers information on magnetic storms and pole reversals.

OOPARTS: *Ancient High Technology.* Web site. Available at *s8int.com/index. html.* Information regarding out-of-place artifacts relevant to the history of the great flood.

"Puma Punko" and "Tiahuanaco." World Mysteries. Web site. Both available at *www.world-mysteries.com.* Reference articles about Puma Punko and Tiahuanaco.

Books

Aivanhov, Omraam Mikhael. *The Symbolic Language of Geometrical Figures.* Frejus, France: Prosveta S.A., 1990.

Braden, Gregg. *Fractal Time: The Secret of 2012 and a New World Age.* Carlsbad, CA: Hay House, 2009.

——. *The Divine Matrix: Bridging Time, Space, Miracles, and Belief.* Carlsbad, CA: Hay House, 2008.

Brennan, Barbara Ann. *Hands of Light: A Guide to Healing Through the Human Energy Field.* New York: Bantam Books, 1988.

Cayce, Edgar. *Atlantis.* Virginia Beach, VA: A.R.E. Press, 2010.

Cayce, Edgar, Gail Cayce Schwartzer, Douglas Richards. *Mysteries of Atlantis.* Virginia Beach, VA: A.R.E. Press, 2007.

Curcio, Kimberly Panisset. *Man of Light.* New York: Select Books, 2002.

Gardner, Laurence. *Bloodline of the Holy Grail.* Gloucester, MA: Fair Winds Trade Press, 2002.

———. *Lost Secrets of the Sacred Ark.* Hammersmith, London: Element (Harper Collins), 2003.

Gray, Henry. *Gray's Anatomy.* 15th edition. New York: Barnes and Nobles Books, 1995.

Kovacs, Maureen Gallery (trans.). *The Epic of Gilgamesh.* Palo Alto, CA: Stanford University Press, 1989. Electronic edition by Wolf Carnahan, 1998. Available online at *www.ancienttexts.org.*

Lipton, Bruce. *The Biology of Belief.* Illustrated edition. Carlsbad, CA: Hay House, 2008.

Losey, Meg Blackburn *Pyramids of Light, Awakening to Multi-Dimensional Awareness.* Andersonville, TN: Spirit Light Resources, 2004.

McTaggart, Lynne. *The Field.* Updated edition. New York: Harper Paperbacks, 2008.

———. *The Intention Experiment.* New York: Free Press, 2008.

Melchizedek, Drunvalo. *The Ancient Flower of Life, Volume 1.* Flagstaff, AZ: Light Technology Publishing, 1998.

———. *The Ancient Flower of Life, Volume 2.* Flagstaff, AZ: Light Technology Publishing, 2000.

The Mystery of 2012: Predictions, Prophecies, and Possibilities. Illustrated edition. Louisville, CO: Sounds True, 2009.

Pert, Candace. *Molecules of Emotion.* New York: Simon & Schuster, 1999.

Pond, Dale. *Universal Laws Never Before Revealed: Keely's Secrets.* Santa Fe, NM: The Message Company, 2000.

Talbot, Michael. *The Holographic Universe.* New York: Harper Collins, 1992.

Wilson, Colin. *From Atlantis to the Sphinx.* New York: Fromm International Publishing, 1997.

Zeyl, Donald J. (trans.). *Plato's Timaeus.* Indianapolis/Cambridge: Hackett Publishing Company, 2000.

Other Sources

Davies, Paul. "A Brief History of the Multiverse." *New York Times*. April 12, 2003. Available at *www.nytimes.com*.

"Einstein Was Right on Gravity's Velocity." *New York Times*. January 8, 2003. Available at *www.nytimes.com*.

Glanz, James. "Studies Suggest Unknown Form of Matter Exists." *New York Times*. July 31, 2002. Available at *www.nytimes.com*.

Lokhorst, Gert-Jan C. "The Originality of Descartes' Theory About the Pineal Gland." *Journal for the History of Neuro Sciences*, 10, no. 1 (2001): 6–18.

MacDonald, G. Jeffrey. "Does the Maya Calendar Predict 2012 Apocalypse?" *USA Today*. March 27, 2007. Available at *www.usatoday.com*.

Miller, Iona, and Richard Allen Miller. "From Helix to Hologram, An Ode on the Human Genome." *Nexus Magazine*, 10, no. 5 (September–October, 2003): 47.

About the Author

 Meg Blackburn Losey, Ph.D. is the author of *The Secret History of Consciousness*, *Parenting the Children of Now*, *Conversations with the Children of Now*, the international bestseller *The Children of Now: Crystalline Children, Indigo Children, Star Kids, Angels on Earth and The Phenomenon of Transitional Children*, *Pyramids of Light: Awakening to Multi-dimensional Reality*, and the *Online Messages*. She is also a contributor to *The Mystery of 2012 Anthology*.

She is a regular columnist for *Kinetics Magazine* and a frequent contributor to numerous other publications.

Dr. Meg is a national and international keynote speaker. She facilitates group journeys to sacred sites in Scotland, England, Ireland, Peru, Bolivia, Egypt, and Mexico. She has also served as a consultant to *Good Morning America* and *20/20*. Dr. Meg can be reached by e-mail at *drmeg@ spiritlite.com* or on her website at *www.spiritlite.com*.

To Our Readers

Weiser Books, an imprint of Red Wheel/Weiser, publishes books across the entire spectrum of occult and esoteric subjects. Our mission is to publish quality books that will make a difference in people's lives without advocating any one particular path or field of study. We value the integrity, originality, and depth of knowledge of our authors.

Our readers are our most important resource, and we appreciate your input, suggestions, and ideas about what you would like to see published. Please feel free to contact us to request our latest book catalog, or to be added to our mailing list.

Red Wheel/Weiser, LLC
500 Third Street, Suite 230
San Francisco, CA 94107
www.redwheelweiser.com